Goetic Evocation

The Magician's Workbook
Volume 2

By
Steve Savedow

MW00697412

Copyright © 1996
by
Steve Savedow

ISBN 1-57353-111-1

Second Printing 1999

EPB-AW-111
an
ESCHATON BOOK
from

ESCHATON™
P R O D U C T I O N S ,   I N C .

60 East Chestnut Street, #236
Chicago, IL 60611

Send a S.A.S.E. for our current catalog!

Visit Eschaton on the Web:
http://www.eschatonbooks.com

TABLE OF CONTENTS

This book is dedicated to the future of Samantha Frost; with thanks to Patti and Tom, Valora and Loren.

Also, thanks to Glen Houghton for his encouragement and assistance.

Special thanks to my wife, Elaine, for her patience and tolerance with my neglectful behaviour during the creative process.

0

INTRODUCTION

As mentioned in the first volume of this series[1], the invocation and the evocation should be considered the two supreme acts of ritual magick. The invocation should be the primary practice of the aspiring practitioner over the first year to eighteen months of study. One should invoke so often, as to nearly allow the activity to dominate their waking hours of existence, either in action, contemplation or reflection. Obviously, the author deems these practices essential to the process of power or energy building, and the individual who exercises in such a manner is duly preparing themselves for a promising future as a ritual magician.

One should invoke the energies of the celestial spheres whenever they draw close to the Earth's orbit, as well as invoking the Lunar energies on every full moon, and perform Solar invocations at noon on at least a bi-weekly basis. Additionally, one should perform banishing rituals[2] on a daily basis, as time allows.[3] "The Invocation of the Bornless One", as described in appendix C of the previous volume, should also be performed regularly. The Eucharist ritual described in chapter 20 of volume one should be performed daily by the aspiring magician, and is likewise an invocational ritual, as are the talismanic rituals outlined in chapter 16 of the first volume.

The practice of ritual evocation however, is a precise and strenuous art. The physical and mental stress would be inconceivable to the unprepared, and any successful attempt of such an act by a novice, would more than likely result in tragedy. The rituals and exercises provided in the first volume of this series should be adapted into one's daily life, for at least the period of one year, and preferably longer, before continuing onto the practice of magickal evocation.

Physical conditioning, as well as spiritual, is an equally essential factor in evocationary work. If not previously conditioned, or naturally very athletic, the novice who plans on practicing the art of ritual evocation should undergo an effective regimen of both endurance and strength building routines. The ideal situation, if at all practical, would be the study of the martial arts, such as Karate or Tae Kwon Do. These arts not only strengthen the physical attributes of the body, but they also sharpen the mental faculties of the mind. If the appropriate conditions for such studies do not exist in your area, it would be advisable to participate in both an aerobic and nautilus program, on an alternating basis, spending at least one hour daily exercising. The aspiring magician should strive to gain the ability to lift two thirds their own body weight to chest level with minimal effort, and to jog five miles in a reasonable time frame.[4]

There is such dramatic differences between the acts of evocation and invocation, that in a sense, they could almost be considered opposites, or at least recognizable as opposing actions. Although a few known and reputable grimoires of significant origin detail various methods of evoking specific and individual entities, the majority of the text of this volume pertains to the system outlined in the "Clavicula Salomonis" or "Key of Solomon"; specifically the "Lemegeton vel Clavicula Salomonis Regis" or "Lesser Key", also sometimes referred to as "The Goetia"[5]. This work defines a system incorporating a relatively complex network of seventy-two "evil spirits", each with recorded individual attributes and properties.

There is always some, or even much suspicion as to the validity of writings of supposedly ancient origin, and "The Key of Solomon" is certainly no exception. It would be impossible for any single person or small group to either verify the authenticity or prove the fraudulence of original manuscripts of medieval origins, such as those possessed by London's British Museum[6]. However, it is the opinion of the author, which was derived from long term experimentation and study of the "Key of Solomon", that the system outlined in the "Lesser Key" does work, although the popular and readily available translation[7], greatly simplifies the matter by not referring back to the "Key of Solomon" for the appropriate preliminaries and precautions. It is hoped that the present volume will rectify the situation by providing an in-depth examination and explanation of the system.

There are a variety of evocationary systems known from early manuscripts, which include John Dee's Enochian system, the system outlined in "The Grimoire of Pope Honourius III", the system of "The Grimoirium Verum"[8], and also of Peter de Abano's "Heptameron", to name a few. The "Goetic" system is very possibly the most dangerous one to work with. Every spirit within the network must be considered evil, and would surely destroy the operator, were it able to.

It is not altogether the author's intention to encourage the practice of magickal evocation, especially "Goetic", as much as to document a bit of his own knowledge on the subject, to aid those with the fortitude to endeavor such a feat. In this day and age, it is not recommended to subject the world and its inhabitants to experience this sort of inferniality. However, for those chosen few who consider themselves worthy, you might first ask yourself, "What if I should happen to succeed?".

1

HIERARCHY

The magickal practitioner who has followed the program outlined in the first volume of this series should move forward in their studies, especially in two fields. The first is the subject of "hierarchy", and the second is "symbology", or study of the occult significance of symbols, which will be discussed in the next chapter. Hierarchy was briefly discussed in the first chapter of the previous volume, although at this point, the subject should be dealt with in greater detail.

Obviously, the subject of hierarchy may be approached in a variety of manners. A textbook definition of hierarchy would be: "1: a division of angels 2: a: a ruling body of clergy organized into orders or ranks, each subordinate to the one above it; specif: the bishops of a province or nation b: church government by a hierarchy 3: a body of persons in authority 4: the classification of a group of people according to ability or to economic, social or professional standing 5: a graded or ranked series".[1] This concept may be applied to all religious, governmental, educational, administrative, political and military authority systems. Even businesses and families are subject to hierarchal outlines, as are the plant and animal kingdoms. The main concern of the ritual magician, however, is that of qabalistic hierarchy.

One of the many possible benefits from study of the qabala is its application as a system of classification. This system may be utilized to describe every existing "thing" from a single atom to our solar system. It also establishes the nature and attributions of the Gods and deities of every belief system, as well as linking various seemingly unrelated correspondences to each deity.

Every culture's mythological and/or religious deities may be classified by qabalistic standards, some of which are outlined in chart #1. It should be noted that these qabalistic classifications are not necessarily an accurate interpretation of the actual status attributed to each deity in the hierarchy of their respective culture. This is merely a convenient manner of associating each with their corresponding counterpart in the various belief systems. The book "777" published by Aleister Crowley[2] is, among other things, a cross reference to deities and their appropriate correspondences. The numerous charts relate specific attributes to the primary deities of the Greeks, Romans, Egyptians, Christian and Hindus, as well as to the numerous Hebrew names

3

given to God. These have been arranged in a "Tree of Life" outline in chart #1. Each of the hierarchal trees or patterns may be best termed as "formulas".

The true and complete hierarchy of the universe might well include every known deity of every known belief system, and would be too vast a network to illustrate on paper. Additionally, the complications of such a composite would be well beyond the means of any mere man to interpret. We can only break the hierarchal patterns down to understandable terms by restricting the comparisons to one belief system at a time.

In order to present a comprehensible and practical depiction of a complex hierarchal network, we will restrict the field to the biblical angelic hierarchy, as related to the qabalistic Solomonic system.[3]

Chart #2 illustrates the formulas of the Archangels and the Orders of Angels.

The qabalistic outline utilized here is the most universal in nature, and explanation of hierarchy is simplified significantly for the benefit of the novice.[4] This system does not necessarily depict an outline of the most powerful to least powerful demi-gods and angelic entities. It simply establishes a pattern of division among the biblical angels and archangels. The divisions do correspond to certain general attributes. These most notably include planetary, elemental, and astrological attributions. In order to incorporate these into the system, we must now complicate matters by introducing several completely different hierarchal formulas.

Chart #3 establishes the planetary dominance of certain Archangels, angels and lesser angelic deities. These may be invoked by use of the invoking hexagrams. The magician would first draw the appropriate hexagram while vibrating the name, ARARITA, and then touching the center of the hexagram while vibrating the name of the specific entity.

The first three aspects of these hierarchies relate to the specific sephiroth, with Saturn corresponding to Binah, Jupiter to Chesed, and so on. The Arch-angel would correspond to the specific sephiroth of the Archetypal world of Atziluth. Then, for example, in order to attract the purest, yet most unstable of the Saturnian energies, one would invoke the Archangel of Binah. The angel of the sephiroth Binah would represent the Saturnian energies of the Briatic or creative world, and one would invoke Cassiel in order to attract it. The intelligence of the sephiroth would be invoked to attract the Yetziric energies, and the spirit for Assiatic energies.

4

The elemental hierarchies are outlined in chart #4. The elemental Archangel of fire would be invoked if one wishes to attract the archetypal energies of fire. The angel Seraph would be invoked in order to attract the Briatic energies of fire. The ruler of the elemental hierarchy may be invoked to attract Yetziric energies. It would be a redundant act to invoke the Assiatic energies of the elements, as they are Assiatic in nature to begin with. The Kings and elementals listed are not angelic beings, although their status in the hierarchy commands a somewhat magickal significance in certain matters.

The elemental angels may be invoked by drawing the appropriate invoking pentagrams, while vibrating the appropriate God-names, and then touching the center of the pentagrams, while vibrating the specific deity's name.

One may ask what possible benefit could all of this information provide for the ritual magician? The combination of knowledge and proper understanding of that knowledge, equals power. This is not political, financial, electrical or even nuclear power. This is magickal power!

We will now introduce the hierarchal formulas for the angels falling under the dominance of the astrological signs. These one hundred and eight angels are divided into eight aspects[5], which are depicted in charts #5 - #9. Each of these formulas represent one of the four qabalistic worlds, incorporating the angels with the twelve signs of the zodiac.

The first or Archetypal world of Atziluth is represented by the twelve angels ruling the houses, as depicted in chart #5. The world of Briah is represented by the twelve lesser assistant angels, as depicted in chart #6. The world of Yetzirah is represented by the twenty four angel lords of the triplicity, which is depicted in chart #7. Chart #8 depicts the thirty six angels of the decanates, representing the world of Assiah, in conjunction with the twenty four rulers of the hours, listed in chart #9, being sixty aspects in all.

Any of these angelic beings may be invoked with the invoking pentagrams, using the elemental representative of the specific sign[6], while vibrating the appropriate God-names. The appropriate astrological sigil should be then drawn in the center of the pentagram, while vibrating the name of the angel to be invoked.

The student is encouraged to seek out any and all available texts which deal with mythological and biblical hierarchies. The subject is of utmost importance, however, the majority of books on the subject were written by individuals possessing little or no education on magickal practices.

Therefore one should attempt to incorporate all given aspects for practical purposes, keeping in mind that much of the available material was likely taken from early translated texts, with great potential for error in transcription. The details should not be accepted as "gospel", unless the references can be verified by several different authorities. Some recommended titles which deal with angelic hierarchy will be listed at the conclusion of this chapter.

According to a variety of religious systems, including Christianity and Judaism, the universe is separated into three realms or "kingdoms"; that of Heaven, Earth and Hell. Heaven is home to angels, Earth to humans, and Hell, of course, is populated by the demons. The demonic hierarchy will be discussed extensively in chapters 4 and 5.

It was mentioned in the first volume that "higher" beings, such as Gods and angels, may be invoked, and "lower" beings, such as spirits and demons, may be evoked. The author neglected to mention that the practitioner is capable of invoking demonic energies, as well as evoking angelic beings to visible appearance. These acts, however, are contrary to currently acceptable behaviour and moral codes, and no positive benefits whatsoever could be achieved by performing them. For that reason, they will not be discussed here. Although, this subject does lead to an interesting topic of conversation. The fact that stimulates this matter is that the two above acts would be classified as acts of "black" magic.

The classification of magickal acts as being either black, white or grey, is a well discussed subject. Although many opinions exist, the determination whether a magickal act falls into these three categories should be made based on the following criteria:

White magick is an act in which the intention and/or results of a ritual affects no being whatsoever, other than the practitioner, and only in a helpful or positive manner.

Grey magick is an act in which the intention and/or results of the ritual affects some being other than the practitioner, but only in a helpful or positive manner.

Black magick is an act in which the intention and/or results of the ritual affects any being in a harmful or negative manner.

If an act of magick results, even accidentally, in harm of any kind to another being, or themselves, the practitioner has (whether willingly or

6

unknowingly) performed the "black art". The karmic reaction will take effect regardless of the intention of the practitioner.

For this reason, the act of invoking demonic energies could only result in the misfortune of the operator, thus bringing harm to themselves, unwittingly or not. The evocation of an angelic being would be harmful to that being. In addition, the sight and strength of presence of angelic entities would prove intolerable to the psyche, as well as the senses, of ninety nine percent of the world's population, inevitably doing some, and possibly great harm to the practitioner making the attempt. Again, an act of black magick, and for these reasons, the topic shall end here. It should be made clear that the author neither endorses nor condones the practice of the "black arts", and would not suggest instructions thereof.

There are those who would contend that, since evocation imprisons the spirit, and considerable threats are directed towards them during interrogation, the act would constitute being one of black magick. This statement would not ring true, should the intention and results of the act not permanently affect another being. If the results somehow have negative effects on another, the act would slip under that dividing line, and the operator would have inadvertently practiced the black art. However, the intention of evocation is frequently of a positive nature, and this act would not fall into the realm of a black operation, until the undesired results manifest. The operator should never intentionally harm the spirit evoked, although these consequences may conceivably result, should the experiment go awry.

For all practical purposes, it should be generally accepted by the student that, as stated in the first chapter of the previous volume, those beings above man on the hierarchal ladder should only be called down by invocation, and those beneath man shall only be summoned up through evocation. No variation of this rule would be considered morally or ethically acceptable, and a strong sense of both morals and ethics should be considered as virtues of great importance and value to the aspiring practitioner of the arts, as well as to any human being.

RECOMMENDED READING

777 (Aleister Crowley)

A Dictionary of Angels (Gustav Davidson)

A Discourse of Angels (George Hammond)

A Treatise of Angels (John Salkeld)

Angels: An Endangered Species (Malcom Godwin)

Angels: The Role of Celestial Beings and Beings of Light (Paola Giovetti)

The Angels (Pascal Parente)

Brotherhood of Angels and Men (Geoffrey Higgins)

Handbook of Angels (H.C. Moolenburgh)

Hierarchies: The Cosmic Ladder of Life (Gertrude Van Pelt)

Hierarchies and the Doctrine of Emanations (G. De Purucker)

Hierarchy of the Blessed Angels (Thomas Heywood)

Kingdom of the Gods (Geoffrey Higgins)

Milton on the Angels (Robert West)

Paradise Lost (John Milton)

CHART #1-A

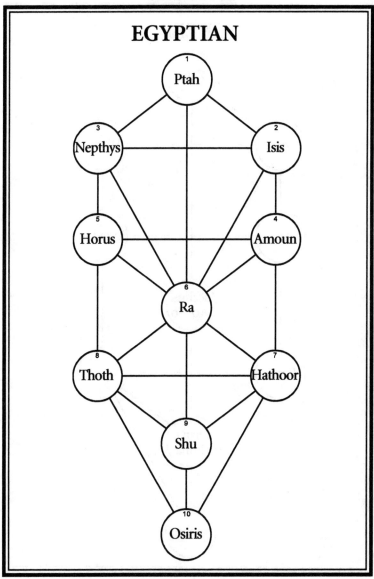

EGYPTIAN

CHART #1-B

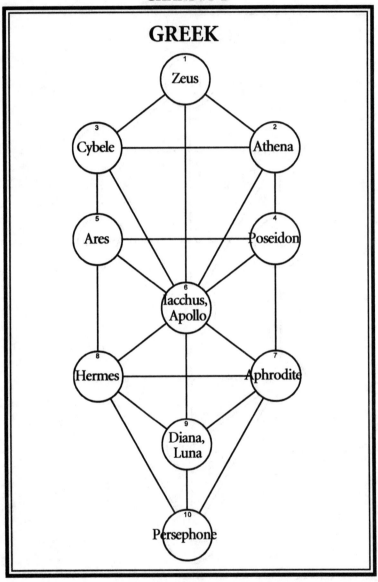

CHART #1-C

HINDU

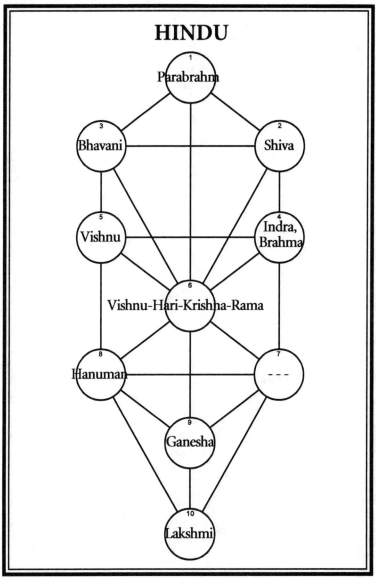

CHART #1-D

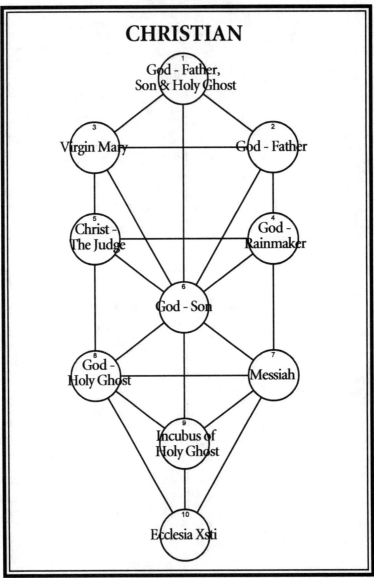

CHRISTIAN

1 God - Father, Son & Holy Ghost

3 Virgin Mary

2 God - Father

5 Christ - The Judge

4 God - Rainmaker

6 God - Son

8 God - Holy Ghost

7 Messiah

9 Incubus of Holy Ghost

10 Ecclesia Xsti

CHART #1-E

PLANETARY

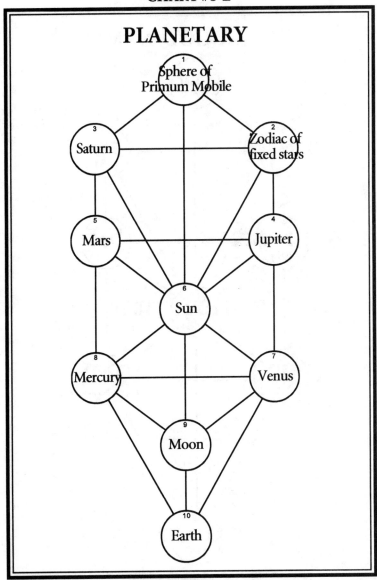

CHART #1-F

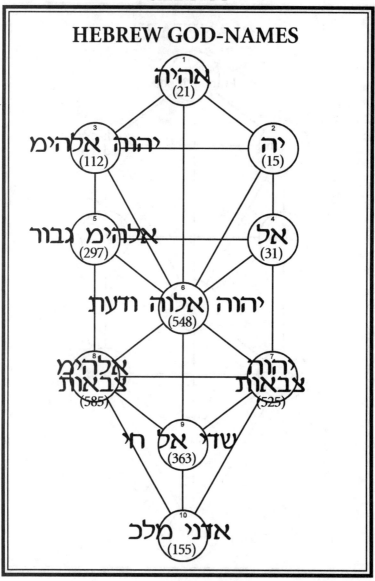

HEBREW GOD-NAMES

1 אהיה (21)

3 יהוה אלהימ (112)

2 יה (15)

5 אלהימ גבור (297)

4 אל (31)

6 יהוה אלוה ודעת (548)

8 אלהימ צבאות (585)

7 יהוה צבאות (525)

9 שדי אל חי (363)

10 אדני מלכ (155)

CHART #2-A

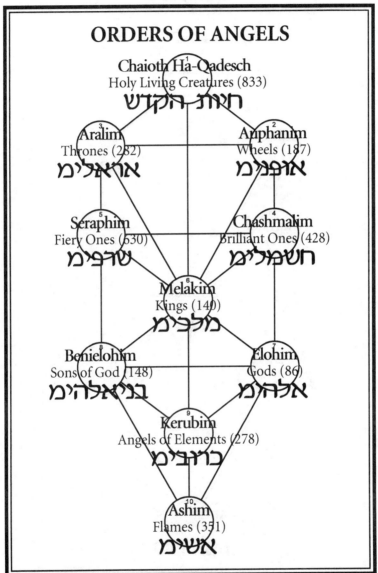

ORDERS OF ANGELS

Chaioth Ha-Qadesch
Holy Living Creatures (833)
חיות הקדש

Aralim
Thrones (282)
אראלים

Auphanim
Wheels (187)
אופנים

Seraphim
Fiery Ones (630)
שרפים

Chashmalim
Brilliant Ones (428)
חשמלים

Melakim
Kings (140)
מלכים

Benielohim
Sons of God (148)
בניאלהים

Elohim
Gods (86)
אלהים

Kerubim
Angels of Elements (278)
כרובים

Ashim
Flames (351)
אשים

CHART #2-B

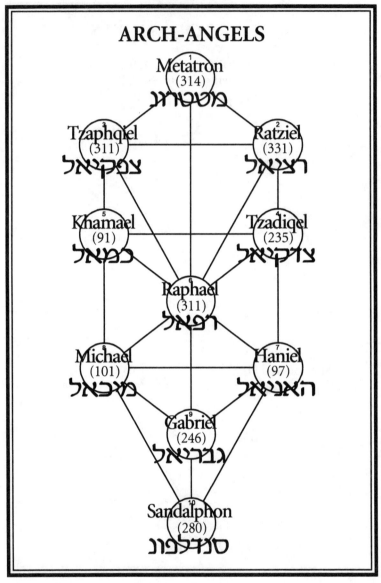

ARCH-ANGELS

Metatron
(314)
מטטרון

Tzaphqiel
(311)
צפקיאל

Ratziel
(331)
רציאל

Khamael
(91)
כמאל

Tzadiqel
(235)
צדקיאל

Raphael
(311)
רפאל

Michael
(101)
מיכאל

Haniel
(97)
האניאל

Gabriel
(246)
גבריאל

Sandalphon
(280)
סנדלפון

Chart #3-A - SATURN	
SEPHIROTH	Binah
HEBREW GOD-NAME	Yehuwau Elohim (112 - יהוה אלהימ)
ARCH-ANGEL (Atziluth)	Tzaphqiel (311 - צפקיאל)
ANGEL (Briah)	Cassiel (361 - כשיאל)
INTELLIGENCE (Yetzirah)	Agiel (45 - אגיאל)
SPIRIT (Assiah)	Zazel (45 - זזאל)

Chart #3-B - JUPITER	
SEPHIROTH	Chesed
HEBREW GOD-NAME	El (31 - אל)
ARCH-ANGEL (Atziluth)	Tzadiqel (235 - צדקיאל)
ANGEL (Briah)	Sachiel (109 - סחיאל)
INTELLIGENCE (Yetzirah)	Iophiel (136 - יהפיאל)
SPIRIT (Assiah)	Hismael (136 - הסמאל)

Chart #3-C - MARS	
SEPHIROTH	Geburah
HEBREW GOD-NAME	Elohim Gibur (297 - אלהימ גבור)
ARCH-ANGEL (Atziluth)	Khamael (91 - כמאל)
ANGEL (Briah)	Zamael (78 - זמאל)
INTELLIGENCE (Yetzirah)	Graphiel (325 - גראפיאל)
SPIRIT (Assiah)	Bartzabel (325 - ברצבאל)

Chart #3-D - SUN	
SEPHIROTH	Tiphareth
HEBREW GOD-NAME	Yehuwau Eloah Veda'ath (548 - יהוה אלוה ודעת)
ARCH-ANGEL (Atziluth)	Raphael (311 - רפאל)
ANGEL (Briah)	Michael (101 - מיכאל)
INTELLIGENCE (Yetzirah)	Therion (666 - תריון)
SPIRIT (Assiah)	Sorath (666 - סורת)

Chart #3-E - VENUS	
SEPHIROTH	Netzach
HEBREW GOD-NAME	Yehuwau Tzbaoth (525 - יהוה צבאות)
ARCH-ANGEL (Atziluth)	Haniel (97 - האניאל)
ANGEL (Briah)	Anael (82 - אנאל)
INTELLIGENCE (Yetzirah)	Hagiel (49 - הגיאל)
SPIRIT (Assiah)	Kademel (175 - קדמאל)

Chart #3-F - MERCURY	
SEPHIROTH	Hod
HEBREW GOD-NAME	Elohim Tzbaoth (585 - אלהימ צבאות)
ARCH-ANGEL (Atziluth)	Michael (101 - מיכאל)
ANGEL (Briah)	Raphael (311 - רפאל)
INTELLIGENCE (Yetzirah)	Tiriel (260 - טיריאל)
SPIRIT (Assiah)	Taphthartharath (2080 - תפתרתרת)

Chart #3-G - MOON	
SEPHIROTH	Yesod
HEBREW GOD-NAME	Shadai El Chai (שדי אל חי - 363)
ARCH-ANGEL (Atziluth)	Gabriel (גבריאל - 246)
ANGEL (Briah)	Gabriel (גבריאל - 246)
INTELLIGENCE OF THE INTELLIGENCES (Yetzirah)	Malkah Be Tarshisim Ve'ad Beruchoth Shecherim (ברוה שהרימ מלכא בתרשישימ ועד -3321)
SPIRIT OF THE SPIRITS (Assiah)	Schad Barschema'ath Ha-Shartathan (שדברשהמעת שרתתנ - 3321)
SPIRIT (Assiah)	Chasmodai (חשמודאי - 369)

Chart #4-A	
HEBREW GOD-NAME	Yehuwau Tzbaoth (525 - יהוה צבאות)
ELEMENT	Fire
DIRECTION	South
SECRET NAME	A'aB (עב - 72)
CARDINAL POINT	Darom (דרום - 250)
ARCHANGEL (Atziluth)	Michael (מיכאל - 101)
ANGEL (Briah)	Seraph (שרפ - 580)
RULER (Yetzirah)	Aral (אראל - 232)
SUPREME KING (Assiah)	Ohooohatan
KING (Assiah)	Djin
ELEMENTALS (Assiah)	Salamanders

Chart #4-B	
HEBREW GOD-NAME	Elohim Tzbaoth (585 - אלהימ צבאות)
ELEMENT	Air
DIRECTION	East
SECRET NAME	Meh (מה - 45)
CARDINAL POINT	Mizrach (מזרח - 255)
ARCHANGEL (Atziluth)	Raphael (רפאל - 311)
ANGEL (Briah)	Ariel (אריאל - 242)
RULER (Yetzirah)	Chassan (חסנ - 118)
SUPREME KING (Assiah)	Tahoeloj
KING (Assiah)	Paralda
ELEMENTALS (Assiah)	Sylphs

Chart #4-C	
HEBREW GOD-NAME	Shadai El Chai (שדי אל חי - 363)
ELEMENT	Water
DIRECTION	West
SECRET NAME	Seg (סג - 63)
CARDINAL POINT	Ma'arob (מערב - 312)
ARCHANGEL (Atziluth)	Gabriel (גבריאל - 246)
ANGEL (Briah)	Tharsis (תרשיס - 970)
RULER (Yetzirah)	Taliahad (טליהד - 58)
SUPREME KING (Assiah)	Thahebyobeaatan
KING (Assiah)	Nichsa
ELEMENTALS (Assiah)	Undines

Chart #4-D	
HEBREW GOD-NAME	Adonai Melech (אדני מלכ - 155)
ELEMENT	Earth
DIRECTION	North
SECRET NAME	Ben (בנ -52)
CARDINAL POINT	Tzaphon (צפונ - 226)
ARCHANGEL (Atziluth)	Auriel (אוריאל - 248)
ANGEL (Briah)	Kerub (כרוב - 228)
RULER (Yetzirah)	Phoriakh (פורלאכ - 337)
SUPREME KING (Assiah)	Thahaaotahe
KING (Assiah)	Ghob
ELEMENTALS (Assiah)	Gnomes

CHART #5 - ANGELS RULING HOUSES (Atziluth)

SIGN	HEBREW	ENGLISH	VALUE
Aries	איאל	Aiel	42
Taurus	טואל	Tual	46
Gemini	גיאל	Giel	44
Cancer	כעאל	Cael	121
Leo	עואל	Ol	107
Virgo	יואל	Voil	47
Libra	יהאל	Jael	46
Scorpio	סוסול	Sosol	162
Sagittarius	סויעסאל	So'ayasel	237
Capricorn	כשויעיה	Casuyoieh	421
Aquarius	אוסיאל	Ausiel	108
Pisces	פשיאל	Pasiel	421

CHART #6 - LESSER ASSISTANT ANGELS (Briah)

SIGN	HEBREW	ENGLISH	VALUE
Aries	שרהיאל	Sharahiel	546
Taurus	ארזיאל	Araziel	249
Gemini	סראיאל	Saraiel	302
Cancer	פכיאל	Pakiel	141
Leo	שרטיאל	Shartiel	550
Virgo	שלתיאל	Shalathiel	771
Libra	חדקיאל	Chedaqiel	153
Scorpio	סאיציאל	Sayetziel	202
Sagittarius	סריטיאל	Saryetiel	320
Capricorn	סמקיאל	Samaqiel	241
Aquarius	צכמקיאל	Tzakemqiel	291
Pisces	וכביאל	Ukabiel	69

CHART #7-A - BY DAY
ANGEL LORDS OF THE TRIPLICITY (Yetzirah)

SIGN	HEBREW	ENGLISH	VALUE
Aries	סטרעטנ	Satera'aton	398
Taurus	ראידאל	Rayediel	246
Gemini	סערש	Sa'arash	630
Cancer	רעדר	Ra'ador	474
Leo	סגהמ	Saghem	108
Virgo	לסלרא	Laselora	321
Libra	תרגבונ	Tharagebon	661
Scorpio	ביתחוי	Bithachoi	436
Sagittarius	אהוז	Ahoz	19
Capricorn	סגדלעי	Sagdala'al	177
Aquarius	עתור	A'athur	676
Pisces	רמרא	Ramra	441

CHART #7-B - BY NIGHT
ANGEL LORDS OF THE TRIPLICITY (Yetzirah)

SIGN	HEBREW	ENGLISH	VALUE
Aries	ספעטאוי	Sapa'tavey	236
Taurus	טוטת	Tuteth	424
Gemini	עוגרמען	A'augarma'an	439
Cancer	עכאל	A'akiel	121
Leo	זלברחית	Zelbrachith	657
Virgo	ססיא	Sasia	131
Libra	אחובראין	Achubrayin	276
Scorpio	סהקנב	Shaqonab	217
Sagittarius	לברמים	Labramim	322
Capricorn	אלויר	Aloyir	247
Aquarius	פלאין	Playin	171
Pisces	נתדוריגאל	Nothadurigiel	704

CHART #8 - ANGELS OF THE DECANATES (Assiah)
(Dec.1 = Ascendant, Dec.2 = Succedent, Dec.3 = Cadent.)

ENGLISH	HEBREW	VALUE	SIGN
1. Zazar	זזר	214	Dec.1 Aries
2. Bahemi	בההמי	62	Dec.2 Aries
3. Satondor	סטנדר	323	Dec.3 Aries
4. Kadomdi	כדמדי	78	Dec.1 Taurus
5. Mancherai	מנחראי	309	Dec.2 Taurus
6. Ikosegnotz	יכסגנוץ	239	Dec.3 Taurus
7. Sagoresh	סגרש	563	Dec.1 Gemini
8. Shahodani	שהדני	369	Dec.2 Gemini
9. Bithon	ביתון	468	Dec.3 Gemini
10. Methraush	מתראוש	947	Dec.1 Cancer
11. Rahidotz	רהדץ	299	Dec.2 Cancer
12. Alinokir	אלינכיר	321	Dec.3 Cancer
13. Losanahar	לוסנהר	351	Dec.1 Leo
14. Zacha'ai	זחעי	95	Dec.2 Leo
15. Sahibor	סהיבר	277	Dec.3 Leo
16. Anonaureh	אננאורה	313	Dec.1 Virgo
17. Rayideh	ראידיה	230	Dec.2 Virgo
18. Mashepor	משפר	620	Dec.3 Virgo

19. Terasani	טרסני	329	Dec.1 Libra
20. Mahornetz	מהרנצ	385	Dec.2 Libra
21. Shachedor	שחדר	512	Dec.3 Libra
22. Kemotz	כמוצ	156	Dec.1 Scorpio
23. Nindohar	נינדוהר	325	Dec.2 Scorpio
24. Uthrodiel	ותרודיאל	657	Dec.3 Scorpio
25. Mishrath	משראת	941	Dec.1 Sagittarius
26. Uherin	והרין	271	Dec.2 Sagittarius
27. Abuha	אבוהא	15	Dec.3 Sagittarius
28. Masnin	מסנין	210	Dec.1 Capricorn
29. Isiseh	יסיסיה	155	Dec.2 Capricorn
30. Isgadibrodiel	יסגדיברודיאל	340	Dec.3 Capricorn
31. Saspom	ססּפמ	240	Dec.1 Aquarius
32. Abadaron	אבדרון	263	Dec.2 Aquarius
33. Garodiel	גרודיאל	254	Dec.3 Aquarius
34. Behelami	בהלמי	87	Dec.1 Pisces
35. Auron	אורון	263	Dec.2 Pisces
36. Saterip	סטריפ	359	Dec.3 Pisces

CHART #9-A - RULERS OF THE HOURS OF THE DAY (AM)

HOUR	ENGLISH	HEBREW	VALUE
1:00	Samael	סמאל	131
2:00	Anael	אנאל	82
3:00	Veguaniel	וגוניאל	106
4:00	Vachmiel	ואחמיאל	96
5:00	Sazquiel	סזקויאל	214
6:00	Samil	סמיל	140
7:00	Barginiel	ברגיניאל	306
8:00	Osagaebial	עסגאביאל	177
9:00	Vadriel	ואדריאל	252
10:00	Oriel	עריאל	311
11:00	Bariel	בריאל	243
12:00	Beratiel	בראטיאל	253

CHART #9-B - RULERS OF THE HOURS OF THE DAY (PM)

HOUR	ENGLISH	HEBREW	VALUE
1:00	Gamiel	גמיאל	84
2:00	Farris	פאריס	351
3:00	Sarquamich	סרקואמיח	425
4:00	Jefischa	יויסחא	95
5:00	Abasdarhon	אבסדארהען	393
6:00	Za'azonash	זעזונאש	441
7:00	Mendrion	מנדריען	424
8:00	Narcoriel	נרכוריאל	517
9:00	Nacoriel	נכוריאל	317
10:00	Jusguarin	יוסגוארין	346
11:00	Dardariel	דרדאריאל	450
12:00	Sarindiel	סרינדיאל	365

2

SYMBOLOGY

The occult significance of symbols is an intricate factor in the practice of high magick. The subject, however, is too vast to present an adequate study in one chapter. It is therefore suggested that the student make concentrated studies of the books listed at the end of this chapter.

Every symbol, whether of magickal or religious origins, represent a certain force or form of energy. Every symbol additionally possesses some quality or qualities, which both attracts a particular energy, and correspondingly repels its opposite. The system utilized by the ritual magician is, again, that of a qabalistic nature.

All letters of every known alphabet could be considered symbols, as well as any word. Most notably, Hebrew letters and words are commonly used on qabalistic magickal weapons and talismans. Additionally, all numbers have occult significance, especially when deduced by qabalistic methods, which is an art known as "Gematria"[1].

Every qabalistic aspect may be depicted not only with a basic number, but also with a simple geometrical figure, which is ultimately a symbolically appropriate representation of the nature of the particular aspect. The ten primary aspects are represented by the figures illustrated in diagram #1.

A circle symbolizes the first sephiroth of Kether, signifying a seemingly empty space. The circle is the most simple and perfect of all geometrical figures, consisting of a single curving line without beginning or end. Even to this day, it is impossible to mathematically calculate the exact dimensions of a circle. The use of the Greek "Pi" $(\pi)^2$ to calculate the area of a circle, although a brilliant and useful formula, is ultimately inadequate as it fails to produce exact results. The dimensions of a circle is destined to remain one of the unknowable secrets of the universe. Its mystery only enhances its ability to most appropriately represent the mysterious sphere of Kether, the supernal mystical force of existence.[3]

The circle is also representative of the "non-number" zero. This is the perfect numerical balance, being the dividing point between the positive and negative numbers. Additionally, any positive number may be reduced to zero by the addition of its equal negative counterpart. It is this reasoning which explains why all numbers are infinite.[4]

A single dot or "point" would also adequately represent Kether. This dot is symbolic of the first "point" of existence, said to be conceived within the "Primum Mobile", "infinite swirlings" or archetypal energy of the primordial supernal sephiroth. The single point where this takes place is indeterminate. There is no possible way for one to focus directly on this, because there exists no confines to its presence. The energy which emanates from this point is continuous and ever present throughout the universe. It is said to be the composite matter for the divine and archetypal force, which man refers to as "God", for it "creates" life, or to be more exact, it is the driving force behind life.

The second sphere of Chokmah is appropriately represented by a single line, which is symbolic of a definite connection between two points, theoretically infinite. This connection links the single point of Kether to that of Chokmah, defining the first qabalistic path, the uniting of the first two supernal forces; that of divine energy or power with ultimate wisdom.

The third supernal force of the sphere named Binah is that of supreme understanding. This sephiroth is represented by an upright equilateral triangle.[5] This figure is symbolic of the "Divine Trinity", being the "Father, Son and the Holy Ghost". The symbol expresses the unification of the three supernal forces of power, wisdom and understanding by the first three qabalistic paths.

The square is representative of the fourth sephiroth named Chesed, which is described by the attributes of mercy, love and majesty. Although the symbolism may not be completely appropriate, a fair depiction of this geometrical figure would be that of two equilateral triangles with a common base line, or positioned with the respective bases overlapping each other.[6] This represents the symbiotic relationship of the upright supernal triangle, which has been described as the "intellectual world", with what Dion Fortune depicts as the "ethical triangle"[7], otherwise described as the "moral world".

Possibly, a more appropriate depiction of the square would be that of four triangles positioned so that each of the four apexes meet in the center of the figure, forming a square which symbolizes a pyramid.[8] This depiction additionally produces a cross within the square, which is a secondary representative of Chesed, being four equal lines joined at the center of the cross. The cross is truly a universal symbol, and its significance is certainly not limited to the Christian religion. This is probably the most ancient symbolic depiction of a human being.

The fifth sephiroth of Geburah, which is described by the attributes of strength and judgement, is represented by the pentagram, or five pointed star. This geometrical figure incorporates enough symbolism to fill the contents of an entire volume in itself. Physically, the symbol consists of five points connected by five lines in a star pattern. This may also be described as being five triangles in a circular pattern, forming a pentagon in the center of the figure.

Symbolically, the pentagram's most universal interpretation is as a depiction of a man (or woman), combining the four elements of fire, air, water and earth, with a fifth aspect, that of human spirit.[9]

In recent times, the pentagram has acquired a rather sinister reputation. This is due to the fact that the symbol is utilized by the modern Satanic movement as their symbolic representation. However, the pentagram is an ancient symbol, the origins of which well pre-date the Catholic and Christian religions, and thus the concept of Satan as being "the devil" or arch-enemy of "God". Much as the Nazis adopted and inverted the Norse "Hammer of Thor" or swastika, the modern satanists have adopted the pentagram, and inverted it so the normally uppermost triangle points downward, suggesting "man" ruled over by the material world[10], rather than the spiritual. Also, with two of the triangles pointing upwards, the symbol depicts the horned head of "Satan".

However, as mentioned earlier, the pentagram is an ancient symbol, which was originally considered to represent such virtues as protection, good health, harmony between the mind and body, good fortune, and most appropriately to the sephiroth Geburah, strength.

The symbol designated to represent the sixth sphere of Tiphareth is the sublime hexagram, or six pointed star. The attributes of this sephiroth include beauty and harmony. The hexagram is composed of an upright equilateral triangle superimposed upon an inverted equilateral triangle. This is symbolic of the complete and perfect unification of the higher supernal triangle with that of the ethical triangle, as earlier discussed. Another depiction of this symbol is that of six triangles positioned in a circular pattern to form a hexagon in its center.

The hexagram was said to be used extensively in magickal operations performed by the Hebrew King Solomon, and for this reason came to be referred to as the "Sigillum Salomonis" or "Seal of Solomon". It was also attributed to Solomon's father, the famed King David, as it was sometimes called the "Scutum David" or the "Shield of David", later to be known as the "Star of David", which today adorns the National flag of Israel.

The heptagram or seven pointed star is the symbolic representative of the sphere of Netzach, whose attributes include victory, love and beauty. This sephiroth is the first aspect of what Dion Fortune designates as the "astral triangle" or "magical world".[11]

The number seven is renowned as being a "lucky" number, but additionally it is highly significant in various religious cultures. For instance, the "Book of Revelations" of the "New Testament" depicts several references to the number seven, including (but not limited to) the book sealed with seven seals (5:1), the seven eyes and horns of the Lamb (5:6), and the seven heads of the Dragon (12:3). In the religious beliefs of medieval Europe, we hear of seven deadly sins, seven virtues, seven sacraments, seven gifts of the Holy Spirit, seven ages of Man, and seven petitions in the Lord's prayer, to name a few examples.

The sephiroth of Hod is represented by the octagram, or eight pointed star, and its attributes include splendour, glory and intellect. The octagram is composed of a square superimposed over another square, which is tilted on end, as depicted by diagram #5, to form an octagon in the center of the design. The symbolism suggests the relationship between the two major qabalistic squares, the first being formed by the spheres of Chockmah, Binah, Chesed and Geburah; and the second square being formed by Chesed, Geburah, Netzach and lastly, Hod.

According to Henry Cornelius Agrippa, the most significant religious symbolism of the number eight refers to the eight ornaments of the priest, being the robe, coat, breast plate, girdle, mitre, ephod[12], a girdle of the ephod, and a plate of gold.[13]

The enneagram or nine pointed star is representative of the sphere of Yesod, the foundation of the qabalistic "Tree of Life", the attributes of which include independence and change. This sephiroth signifies the third aspect of the third qabalistic world, which is known as the "astral triangle" or "magical world", as earlier stated.

The number nine is mathematically the square of the number three, which offers a multitude of symbolisms relating to those of the triangle, being that Yesod represents the apex of the third qabalistic triangle. The number nine also signifies the nine orders of blessed angels, once again according to Agrippa, being the Seraphim, Cherubim, Thrones, Dominations, Powers, Virtues, Principalities, Archangels and Angels.[14]

The tenth sephiroth of Malkuth is represented by a circle divided by an X within its confines, symbolizing the earth composed of the four elements of fire, air, water and earth. The circle signifies the characteristics of the first sephiroth of Kether manifested in Malkuth, for as it is written upon on the "Emerald Tablet" of Hermes Trisgemistus, "True and without error, certain and most true; That which is above is like that which is below, and that which is below is like that which is above.". Another phrase befitting to describe this relationship is the qabalistic axiom, "Malkuth is within Kether, as Kether is in Malkuth".

After discussing the ten primary aspects of the qabalistic "Tree of Life", it is appropriate to continue on to the twenty two secondary aspects, or "paths", of the tree, which are illustrated in diagram #6. Each of these paths represent specific attributes and virtues which correspond to known astrological and elemental aspects. Accordingly, the corresponding astrological and elemental sigils are utilized to represent these paths, as depicted in chart #10. Each of these symbols suggest a myriad of interpretation, which are best studied in the qabalistic texts recommended in chapter 11 of the previous volume, and those texts listed at the conclusion of this chapter.

Also depicted in chart #10 are the twenty two Tarot trumps or "Atu's", each of which represent one of the qabalistic paths. The symbolisms of the Tarot trumps suggest direct relationships with the paths of the "Tree of Life", and are in fact, considered "keys" through which one might gain access to their mysteries.[15]

The twenty two Hebrew letters may also be considered sigils, and each letter also represents one of the paths, as additionally depicted in chart #10. Qabalistically, the letters have specific interpretations attributed to them, as listed in appendix A of the previous volume.

Although thus far, we have barely breached the subject of symbology, the remainder of this chapter will deal with the talismans of "The Key of Solomon the King", first translated into English by Samuel L. MacGregor-Mathers in 1888. The student is then urged to make serious studies of the texts listed at the conclusion of this chapter.

The talismans of "The Key of Solomon", which are presented in chart #11, must be charged by invoking the planetary forces, in the manner described in chapter 16 of the previous volume. Additionally, several other requirements for these talismans are listed in Book I, chapter XVIII of the "Key", as follows:

These Pentacles are usually made of the metal most suitable to the nature of the Planet; and then there is no occasion to observe the rule of particular colors. They should be engraved with the instrument of Art in the days and hours proper to the Planet.

Saturn ruleth over Lead; Jupiter over Tin; Mars over Iron; the Sun over Gold; Venus over Copper; Mercury over the mixture of Metals; and the Moon over Silver.

They may also be made with exorcised virgin paper, writing thereon with the colours adopted for each Planet, referring to the rules already laid down in the proper Chapters, and according to the Planet with which the Pentacle is in sympathy.

Wherefore unto Saturn the colour of Black is appropriate; Jupiter ruleth over Celestial Blue; Mars over Red; the Sun over Gold, or the colour of Yellow or Citron; Venus over Green; Mercury over Mixed Colours; the moon over Silver, or the colour of Argentine Earth.

The Matter of which the Pentacle is constructed should be Virgin, never having been used for any other purpose; or if it be metal it should be purified by fire.

As regards the size of the Pentacles it is arbitrary, so long as they are made according to the rules, and with the requisite solemnities, as hath been ordained.

The virtues of the Holy Pentacles are no less advantageous unto thee than the knowledge of the secrets which I have already given unto thee; and thou shouldest take particular care if thou makest them upon virgin parchment to use the proper colours; and if thou engravest them upon metal, to do so in the manner taught thee; and so shalt thou have the satisfaction of seeing them produce the promised effect. But seeing that this Science is not a Science of argument and open reasoning, but that, on the contrary, it is entirely mysterious and occult, we should not argue and deliberate over these matters, and it is sufficient to believe firmly to enable us to bring into operations that which hath already been taught.

When thou shalt construct these Pentacles and Characters, it is necessary never to forget the Incense, nor to employ anything beyond that of which mention is made.

It is necessary, above all things, to be attentive to the operation, and never to forget or omit those things which contribute to the success which the Pentacles and Experiments promise, having ever in thy mind no other intention than the Glory of God, the accomplishment of thy desires, and loving-kindness towards thy neighbour.

Each of these talismans are designated for certain specific purposes, which correspond to the attributes of the ruling planet. The Saturnian talismans are used for such matters as striking terror into and chasing away spirits, and for executing operations of ruin, destruction and death. The Jupiterian talismans are used to acquire glory, riches and tranquility of mind, and for protection against spirits. The Martian talismans are used for protection against diseases and enemies, as well as exciting war and hostility. The Solar talismans are used to command obedience of all creatures, to acquire renown and glory, and for operations of invisibility. The Venutian talismans are used for obtaining grace and honour, and also to attract love. Mercurial talismans are used to cause spirits to answer questions truly, as well as to acquire knowledge and understanding. The Lunar talismans are used as protection against all dangers by water, to excite or cause heavy rains, and defend against all forms of evil sorceries.

The possession of an arsenal of Solomonic talismans would prove invaluable to the practitioner of the art. As earlier stated, these should be charged in the manner described in Chapter 16 of the previous volume, during the appropriate days and hours specified in the tables depicted in chart #12. Additionally, the appropriate archangel and angel, as designated in chart #13, should be invoked prior to the charging ritual.

The acquisition of true virgin parchment would be a virtual impossibility in this day and age, therefore metal disks would be the most feasible choice of materials. Other than gold, these should be economically reasonable, and since the size of these talismans is arbitrary, small thin gold disks should not command too exorbitant of a cost. The use of a common metal scribe tool, which are available in most hardware stores, would be effective for engraving the disks.

When carrying these talismans, they should be wrapped in natural cloth, such as cotton or silk, in the color appropriate to the ruling planet, and kept in an appropriately colored pouch, also made of natural cloth..

Talismanic magic is an extremely useful, efficient and practical system, which unfortunately, is often neglected by modern practitioners. The use of this system offers a potentially infinite range of possibilities, which could only prove extremely beneficial to the magician. In order to acquire an adequate knowledge in the field of talismanic magic, it should be considered essential to properly educate oneself in the field of symbology, and the most effective manner to do so would be with an in-depth study of the serious texts available on the subject. Several suggestions are presented here, and others will be found referred to throughout these works.

RECOMMENDED READING

777 & Other Qabalistic Writings (Aleister Crowley)

Ancient, Pagan and Modern Christian Symbolism (Thomas Inman)

Cosmic Symbolism (Sephariel)

Dictionary of Alchemical, Hermetic and Alchemical Sigils (Fred Gettings)

Dictionary of Symbols (J.E. Cirlott)

Dictionary of Symbols (Hans Biedermann)

Herder Dictionary of Symbols (English translation by Boris Matthews)

Kabala of Numbers (Sephariel)

Lost Language of Symbology (Harold Bayley)

Occult Power of Numbers (W. Wynn Westcott)

Occult Signs and Symbols (Rudolph Steiner)

Practical Guide to Qabalistic Symbolism (Gareth Knight)

Secret Teachings of All Ages (Manly Hall)

Symbols, Signs and Signets (E. Lehner)

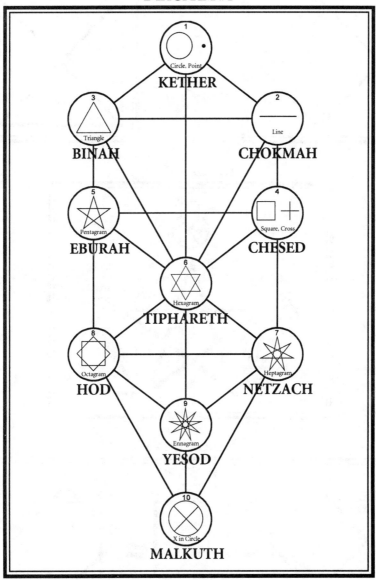

DIAGRAM #1

DIAGRAM #2

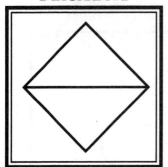

DIAGRAM #3

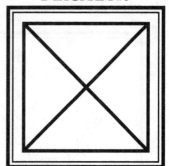

DIAGRAM #4

DIAGRAM #5

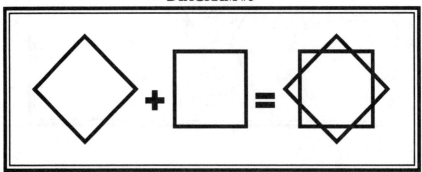

DIAGRAM #6

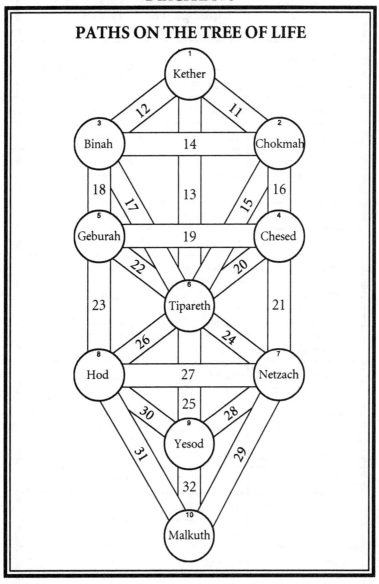

PATHS ON THE TREE OF LIFE

CHART #10
REPRESENTATIVE SYMBOLS OF THE QABALISTIC PATHS

Paths	Astrological & Elemental sigils	Tarot Trumps
11. Aleph - א	Air - △	Fool
12. Beth - ב	Mercury - ☿	Magus
13. Gimel - ג	Luna - ☽	High Priestess
14. Daleth - ד	Venus - ♀	Empress
15. Heh - ה	Aries - ♈	Emperor
16. Vau - ו	Taurus - ♉	Hierophant
17. Zayin - ז	Gemini - Ⅱ	Lovers
18. Cheth - ח	Cancer - ♋	Chariot
19. Teth - ט	Leo - ♌	Strength
20. Yodh - י	Virgo - ♍	Hermit
21. Kaph - כ	Jupiter - ♃	Wheel of Fortune
22. Lamed - ל	Libra - ♎	Justice
23. Mem - מ	Water - ▽	Hanged Man
24. Nun - נ	Scorpio - ♏	Death
25. Samekh - ס	Sagittarius - ♐	Temperance
26. Ayin - ע	Capricorn - ♑	Devil
27. Peh - פ	Mars - ♂	Tower
28. Tzaddi - צ	Aquarius - ♒	Star
29. Qoph - ק	Pisces - ♓	Moon
30. Resh - ר	Sol - ☉	Sun
31. Shin - ש	Fire - △	Angel
32. Tau - ת	Saturn - ♄	Universe

CHART #11-A[16]
TALISMANS OF THE "KEY OF SOLOMON"

Pentacles of Saturn

1.

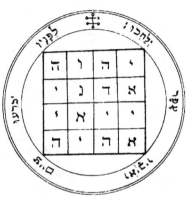

2.

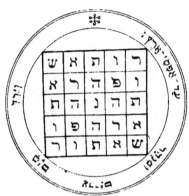

3.

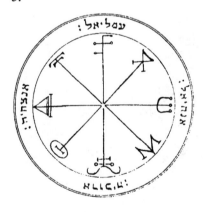

4.

5.

6.

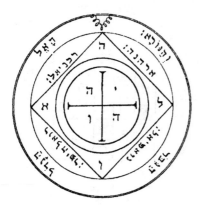

7.

CHART #11-B
TALISMANS OF THE "KEY OF SOLOMON"

Pentacles of Jupiter

1.

2.

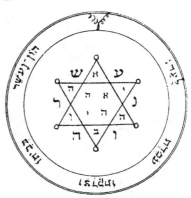

3.

4.

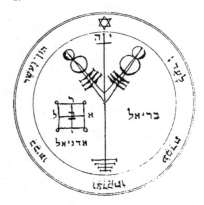

5.

6.

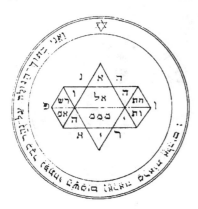

7.

CHART #11-C
TALISMANS OF THE "KEY OF SOLOMON"

Pentacles of Mars

1.

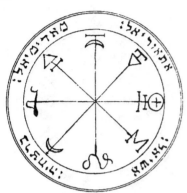

2.

3.

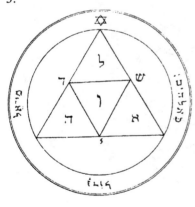

4.

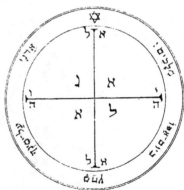

5.

6.

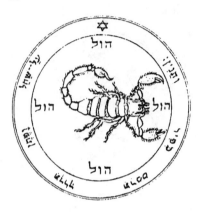

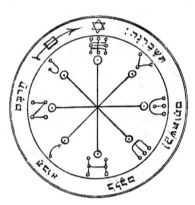

7.

CHART #11-D
TALISMANS OF THE "KEY OF SOLOMON"

Pentacles of the Sun

1.

2.

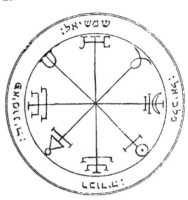

3.

4.

5.

6.

7.

CHART #11-E
TALISMANS OF THE "KEY OF SOLOMON"

Pentacles of Venus

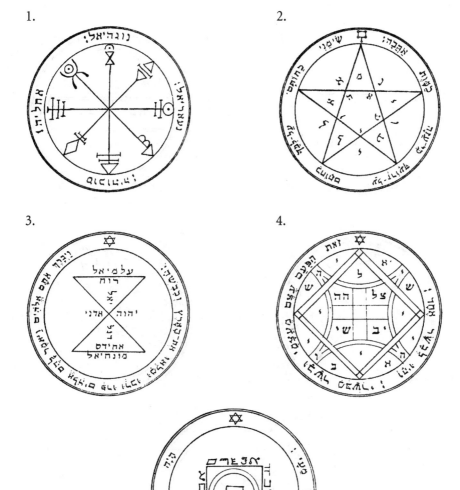

1.

2.

3.

4.

5.

CHART #11-F
TALISMANS OF THE "KEY OF SOLOMON"

Pentacles of Mercury

1.

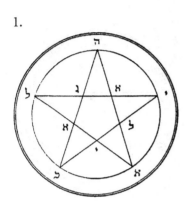

2.

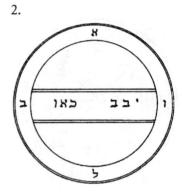

3.

4.

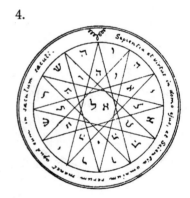

5.

CHART #11-G
TALISMANS OF THE "KEY OF SOLOMON"

Pentacles of the Moon

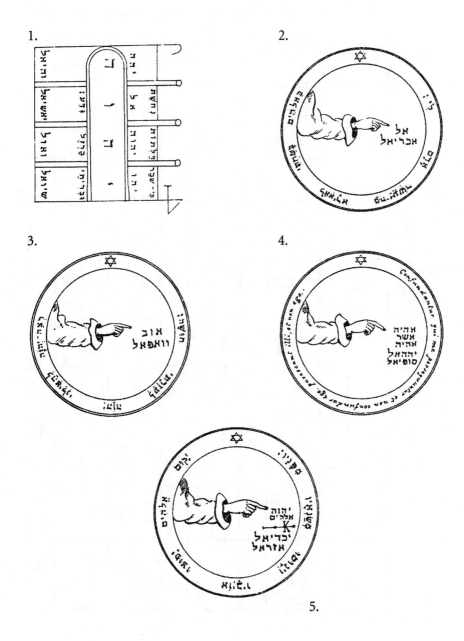

1.

2.

3.

4.

5.

CHART # 12

TABLE OF THE PLANETARY HOURS

Sunday	Monday	Tuesday	Wednesday	Hours from Sunset to Sunset	Hours from Midnight to Midnight	Thursday	Friday	Saturday
Mercury	Jupiter	Venus	Saturn	8	1	Sun	Moon	Mars
Moon	Mars	Mercury	Jupiter	9	2	Venus	Saturn	Sun
Saturn	Sun	Moon	Mars	10	3	Mercury	Jupiter	Venus
Jupiter	Venus	Saturn	Sun	11	4	Moon	Mars	Mercury
Mars	Mercury	Jupiter	Venus	12	5	Saturn	Sun	Moon
Sun	Moon	Mars	Mercury	1	6	Jupiter	Venus	Saturn
Venus	Saturn	Sun	Moon	2	7	Mars	Mercury	Jupiter
Mercury	Jupiter	Venus	Saturn	3	8	Sun	Moon	Mars
Moon	Mars	Mercury	Jupiter	4	9	Venus	Saturn	Sun
Saturn	Sun	Moon	Mars	5	10	Mercury	Jupiter	Venus
Jupiter	Venus	Saturn	Sun	6	11	Moon	Mars	Mercury
Mars	Mercury	Jupiter	Venus	7	12	Saturn	Sun	Moon

Sun	Moon	Mars	Mercury	8	1	Jupiter	Venus	Saturn
Venus	Saturn	Sun	Moon	9	2	Mars	Mercury	Jupiter
Mercury	Jupiter	Venus	Saturn	10	3	Sun	Moon	Mars
Moon	Mars	Mercury	Jupiter	11	4	Venus	Saturn	Sun
Saturn	Sun	Moon	Mars	12	5	Mercury	Jupiter	Venus
Jupiter	Venus	Saturn	Sun	1	6	Moon	Mars	Mercury
Mars	Mercury	Jupiter	Venus	2	7	Saturn	Sun	Moon
Sun	Moon	Mars	Mercury	3	8	Jupiter	Venus	Saturn
Venus	Saturn	Sun	Moon	4	9	Mars	Mercury	Jupiter
Mercury	Jupiter	Venus	Saturn	5	10	Sun	Moon	Mars
Moon	Mars	Mercury	Jupiter	6	11	Venus	Saturn	Sun
Saturn	Sun	Moon	Mars	7	12	Mercury	Jupiter	Venus

CHART #13-A

The Table of the Magical Names of the Hours, and of the Angels who rule them, commencing at the first hour after Midnight of each day, and ending the ensuing midnight. Part A - Midnight through Midday.

Hours	Sunday	Monday	Tuesday	Wednesday	Thursday	Friday	Saturday
1. Yayn	Raphael	Sachiel	Anael	Cassiel	Michael	Gabriel	Zamael
2. Yanor	Gabriel	Zamael	Raphael	Sachiel	Anael	Cassiel	Michael
3. Nasnia	Cassiel	Michael	Gabriel	Zamael	Raphael	Sachiel	Anael
4. Salla	Sachiel	Anael	Cassiel	Michael	Gabriel	Zamael	Raphael
5. Sadedali	Zamael	Raphael	Sachiel	Anael	Cassiel	Michael	Gabriel
6. Thamur	Michael	Gabriel	Zamael	Raphael	Sachiel	Anael	Cassiel
7. Ourer	Anael	Cassiel	Michael	Gabriel	Zamael	Raphael	Sachiel
8. Thaine	Raphael	Sachiel	Anael	Cassiel	Michael	Gabriel	Zamael
9. Neron	Gabriel	Zamael	Raphael	Sachiel	Anael	Cassiel	Michael
10. Yayon	Cassiel	Michael	Gabriel	Zamael	Raphael	Sachiel	Anael
11. Abai	Sachiel	Anael	Cassiel	Michael	Gabriel	Zamael	Raphael
12. Nathalon	Zamael	Raphael	Sachiel	Anael	Cassiel	Michael	Gabriel

CHART #13-B

The Table of the Magical Names of the Hours, and of the Angels who rule them, commencing at the first hour after Midnight of each day, and ending the ensuing midnight. Part B - Midday through Midnight.

Hours	Sunday	Monday	Tuesday	Wednesday	Thursday	Friday	Saturday
1. Beron	Michael	Gabriel	Zamael	Raphael	Sachiel	Anael	Cassiel
2. Barol	Anael	Cassiel	Michael	Gabriel	Zamael	Raphael	Sachiel
3. Thanu	Raphael	Sachiel	Anael	Cassiel	Michael	Gabriel	Zamael
4. Athor	Gabriel	Zamael	Raphael	Sachiel	Anael	Cassiel	Michael
5. Mathon	Cassiel	Michael	Gabriel	Zamael	Raphael	Sachiel	Anael
6. Rana	Sachiel	Anael	Cassiel	Michael	Gabriel	Zamael	Raphael
7. Netos	Zamael	Raphael	Sachiel	Anael	Cassiel	Michael	Gabriel
8. Tafrac	Michael	Gabriel	Zamael	Raphael	Sachiel	Anael	Cassiel
9. Sassur	Anael	Cassiel	Michael	Gabriel	Zamael	Raphael	Sachiel
10. Agla	Raphael	Sachiel	Anael	Cassiel	Michael	Gabriel	Zamael
11. Caerra	Gabriel	Zamael	Raphael	Sachiel	Anael	Cassiel	Michael
12. Salam	Cassiel	Michael	Gabriel	Zamael	Raphael	Sachiel	Anael

CHART #14

The Table of the Archangels, Angels, Metals, Days of the Week, and Colours attributed to each Planet.

Days	Saturday	Thursday	Tuesday	Sunday	Friday	Wednesday	Monday
Archangel	Tzaphqiel	Tzadiqel	Khamael	Raphael	Haniel	Michael	Gabriel
Angel	Cassiel	Sachiel	Zamael	Michael	Anael	Raphael	Gabriel
Planet	Saturn	Jupiter	Mars	Sun	Venus	Mercury	Moon
Metal	Lead	Tin	Iron	Gold	Copper	Mercury	Silver
Colour	Black	Blue	Red	Yellow	Green	Purple or Mixed Colours	White

3

A BRIEF HISTORY OF "THE KEY OF SOLOMON"

An attempt to trace the origins of the provocative manuscripts entitled "The Key of Solomon" would inevitably prove fruitless. A fair amount of information is on record dating back to the fourteenth century pertaining to the text; however those centuries in which the vast majority of the western population sought out and destroyed any literature that contradicted their relatively new found beliefs of Catholicism and Christianity, marked the loss of virtually aeons of valuable occult lore. Any manuscript, regardless of historical value, which dealt with such matters as the "summoning of spirits" would doubtless have been subject to the flame during that barbarous era, as likely would have been the possessor of such literature.

As briefly mentioned in the introduction, several existing manuscripts have survived, mainly in European libraries and museums. Each has minor differences, and certain separate manuscripts were entitled "Lemegeton vel Clavicula Salomonis Regis", which translates "Little" or "Lesser Key of Solomon the King". Contrary to the invocational matter included in "The Key of Solomon", or "Clavicula Salomonis", this second manuscript dealt exclusively with the evocation of "evil spirits".

Some interesting conjecture regarding the antiquity of "The Key of Solomon" are discussed in Richard Cavendish's "A History of Magic"[1]. In chapter two, Cavendish mentions that King Solomon existed in the tenth century B.C., and was the most powerful of Jewish kings. He also remarks that Solomon had "...an appetite for foreign women and strange gods, which gave his character a strange cast". He goes on to say "Legend has it that magical texts written by Solomon, or by the demons under his control, were banned by King Hezekiah of Judah, about 700 B.C.".

Cavendish later states that, "A 'Livre de Solomon', with instructions for invoking demons was burned about 1350 on the orders of Pope Innocent VI. A 'Clavicula Salomonis' (Key or Little Key of Solomon) and a 'Sigillum Salomonis' (Seal of Solomon) are mentioned in a pamphlet of 1456, addressed to the Duke of Burgundy,...". Obviously, this background information remains sporadic, leaving a gap of some two thousand years unaccounted for; although few actual handwritten manuscripts on any subject survive over periods of five hundred years, due to the natural decaying process of ink and paper, as well as the poor quality of most materials used in these impoverished times.[2] This fact unfortunately reduces any likelihood of finding "hard evidence" existing previously to medieval times.

However, this fact has not deterred certain notable scholars from voicing their own opinions regarding "The Key of Solomon". In chapter one of "The Secret Lore of Magic"[3], Idries Shah notes that in 1559, according to the "Inquisition Records of Toledo and Cuenca"[4], the Spanish inquisition prohibited "The Key of Solomon" as a dangerous book. Shah also mentions his belief that it has existed from very remote antiquity, in one form or another, possibly from Semetic, or even Babylonian origins.[5]

Emile Grillotte De Givry (1874-1929), in book one, chapter eight of "Witchcraft, Magic and Alchemy"[6], states "Nevertheless, the tradition which attributes the first idea of this manual ("Key of Solomon") of sorcery to Solomon is not perhaps so devoid of foundation as one might suppose; the tradition goes back at least to a very remote antiquity.".

He later offers some interesting historical information on Solomon himself: "But the memory of all this pomp and profusion, so well calculated to beguile the imagination of Asiatics, has not been preserved for us by the bible alone.[7] The famous Persian poet, Firdausi, wrote his history in verse, under the title of 'Suleiman-Nameh'." He then states:

> "...Solomon, Son of David, otherwise 'Suleiman-ibn-Daoud', becomes a legendary personage without equal in any literature, even in the glowing fictions of India. Not only is he the richest and wisest monarch on earth, but his knowledge has made him the most powerful of men, and he commands all celestial, terrestrial, and infernal spirits; he is obeyed by the subterranean pigmies and gnomes, and by undines, elves and, salamanders.
>
> The author of the Arabic book 'Tarikh-mon-Te-Kheh' reports that he mounted the throne at twelve years of age, and that God subjected to him the jinn - that is to say, good and evil spirits - as well as the birds and winds. The three realms of nature obeyed him likewise, and the very plants taught him their properties.
>
> In the palace paved with crystal Solomon had the jinn and the demons seated at tables of iron, the poor at tables of wood, chiefs of armies at tables of silver, and learned men and doctors of the law at tables of gold, and then last he served himself. According to the Koran, the jinn worked under his eyes, building palaces and making statues, gardens, ponds, and precious carpets. When he desired to visit distant lands he travelled carried upon their backs."

He then presents some antiquarian detail as to the book itself:

"Whatever we may think of these legends, in the first century of the Christian era, at the time of Vespasian, a book of incantations for summoning demons was already in circulation under the name of Solomon. The historian Flavius Josephus, who was contemporaneous with this epoch, says that the book was in the hands of a Jew named Eleazer, who, in Vespasian's presence, delivered those possessed by devils by applying to their nose a ring chased with a figure of a root designed by Solomon for this purpose; he recited at the same time the words set down by Solomon in this book. With fresh formulas added to it in the course of time, this work may possibly have been the embryo of our present 'Clavicula de Salomon'.

From that time onward we continually see Solomon's books of sorcery mentioned by various authors all down the ages. In the eleventh century the Greek writer Michael Psellus speaks of the treatise on stones and demons composed by Solomon. Another Byzantine historian of the thirteenth century, Nicetas Choniates, in Book IV, paragraph 7, of his history of the Emperor Manuel Comnenus, makes mention of a book which can only be the 'Clavicula de Salomon'; it was in the hands of Aaron Isaac, interpreter to the Emperor, and he says that 'he who should read it could cause legions of demons to appear'."

In chapter four of "The History of Magic" by Eliphas Levi[8], Levi states "The popular tradition of magic affirms that he who possesses the Keys of Solomon can communicate with spirits of all grades and can exact obedience on the part of all natural forces. These keys, so often lost, and as often recovered, are no other than the talismans of the seventy two names and the mysteries of the thirty two hieroglyphic paths, reproduced by the Tarot. By the aid of these signs and by their infinite combinations, which are like those of numbers and letters, it is possible to arrive at the natural and mathematical revelation of all secrets of nature, and it is this sense that communication is established with the whole hierarchy of intelligence."

One opposing viewpoint is that of the noteworthy scholar Arthur E. Waite, whose text "The Book of Ceremonial Magic"[9] was highly recommended in the previous volume of this series. Much of Waite's dialogue attempts to discount the credulity of "The Key of Solomon's" antiquity, although he himself states "I do not propose to be the historian of magic, white or black, or the classifier of its MSS.". He goes on to insult S.L. MacGregor-Mathers, the first English translator of "The Key of Solomon"[10], for not omitting some of the more distasteful portions in his translation[11], and Waite further condemns his ritual magick practices.[12]

A footnote in chapter three of "The Book of Ceremonial Magic" lists some valuable historical manuscript information, stating "'Les Clavicules de Rabbi Salomon', 2346 (72 S.A.F.), claims to be literally translated from the Hebrew text into French. 2348 (75 S.A.F.) is entitled 'Livre de la Clavicule de Salomon, Roy des Herbreux'; it is said to have been translated from the Hebrew into Italian by Abraham Clorno, and thence into French. 2349 (77 S.A.F.) reads 'Les Vraies Clavicules du Roy Salomon, traduitte (sic) de l'Hebreux par Armadel'. 2350 (78 S.A.F.) is entitled 'Le Secret des Secrets, autrement La Clavicule de Salomon, ov le Veritable Grimoire'. Finally, there is the 'Livre Second de la Clavicule de Salomon', 2791 (76 S.A.F.)."

Specifically on "The Lemegeton" or "Lesser Key", Waite states "About its antiquity there is no need for serious dispute; it claims to be translated from the Hebrew, but its earliest perfect examples are in French of the seventeenth century, and no one has heard of the original; it must have existed, however, in a much earlier form; it is the subject of continual reference by demonologists like Wierus[13] under the style of the Sorcerer's 'Liber Spirituum', and it is from this source that the scornful sceptic who was the pupil of Agrippa, derived his 'Pseudo-Monarchia Damonum', with, however, significant variations from the known copies." Afterwards, Waite finally does concede that "It is indeed, by no means improbable that the first or Goetic portion constitutes the true 'Lemegeton', and that the other sections, apparently unknown to Wierus, are additions of a later date."[14]

It should be noted that neither Waite, nor any occult scholar or historian, has ever provided evidence verifying the fraudulence of this famous grimoire, and the circumstantial evidence supporting its claim to antiquity is substantial.[15]

The circumstances surrounding the relatively recent first English printing of the "Goetia"[16] was, as should be expected, quite controversial. Normally attributed to Aleister Crowley, the book was actually translated by S.L. MacGregor-Mathers, with only a few footnotes and introduction added by Crowley.

In chapter three of the Crowley biography written by Francis King, "The Magical World of Aleister Crowley"[17], King mentions a "magical war" being waged between Crowley and MacGregor-Mathers, and some detail as to the translation of "The Goetia": "Mathers's assaults ended and Crowley lost his resumed interest in ceremonial magic. Before he did so however he issued a pirated edition of Mathers's version of the 'Goetia' to which he prefaced a note claiming that Mathers had 'succumbed unhappily to the assaults of the 'Four Great Princes' (acting notably under Martial influences)' and that Mathers and his wife had had their own souls displaced by those two occult charlatans who called themselves Mr. and Mrs. Horos and had been engaging in running a bogus occult order in London's Gower Street."

This edition has been reprinted often over the years, most notably by the DeLaurence Publishing Company, and most recently by Magickal Childe Publishing Company. Also, the Health Research Company of Mokelumne Hill, CA has been producing an inexpensive spiral bound facsimile (xeroxed) edition for many years. In fact, on today's antiquarian book market, "Goetia" reprints are considered fairly common. Additionally, several other English translations have surfaced over the last few decades. Nelson and Ann White have translated the entire five sections of the "Lemegeton: Clavicula Salomonis", published by the Technology Group of Fremont, California in 1983. Also, Heptangle Books of Berkeley Heights, New Jersey had published a free rendering of the "Lemegeton" under the title "A Book of Spirits", in 1972.[18] It is highly recommended that the student acquire an English translation of "The Lesser Key of Solomon" for comparison use with the rest of this text.

ILLUSTRATION OF BACK COVER OF EQUINOX V1 #4, 1ST ED.
AD FOR GOETIA

PRICE
ONE
GUINEA
NET

To be had
of The Equinox,
124 Victoria St., S.W.
and through all
Booksellers

GOETIA vel Clavicula

SALOMONIS REGIS

(The Lesser Key of Solomon the King.)

The best, simplest, most intelligible and most effective
treatise extant on

CEREMONIAL MAGIC

Careful and complete instruction ; ample illustration ;
beautiful production. This book is very much easier
both to understand and to operate than the so-called
"Greater" Key of Solomon.

ONLY A FEW COPIES REMAIN FOR SALE.

4

THE QLIPHOTH

The experiences and recorded experiments conducted by the author lead him to the conclusion that the "Lesser Key of Solomon" is at least, based in reality. The spirits attributed to the "Goetia" correspond appropriately to specific aspects of the "Qliphothic" system, which is in actuality, an integral counterpart to the Qabalistic. This is to be expected, as the magickal system employed by Solomon was qabalistically based.

If the student has sufficiently studied the qabalistic texts recommended in chapter 11 of the previous volume, they should have at least a minute knowledge of the qliphoth's presence, and necessity of existence. The subject of qabalah is considered a rather obscure topic among conventional scholars, and even among those unconventional few, the qliphothic matter is considered equally as obscure again.

Very little has been written specifically on the magickal aspects of the qliphoth. In fact, it's study is strongly discouraged by the great majority of teachers of ritual magick. The mere mention of its name seems to strike some instinctive fear in the so-called qabalists of this century, which befits an age old axiom to be quoted here: "Man only fears that which he does not understand."

A growing craze currently experiencing an upsurge of popularity in the occult community is the practice of "chaos" magick. Many exuberant and youthful ritual magicians are tending to restrict themselves to the study of "chaos", as if it were a complete system in itself, when actually it is nothing more than a part of the qabalistic ritual magick system.

This is absolutely not to suggest that this part should be ignored or neglected. On the contrary, one who neglects it or refuses to acknowledge its existence, is equally as unbalanced as those who neglect the qabalistic. The true qabalist should realize that the qliphoth is intricately interwoven with the qabala, and is actually its essential dualistic counterpart. After a working knowledge of the "Tree of Life" is established, the student should proceed logically and scientifically with qliphothic studies.

The last section of the MacGregor-Mathers translation of "The Key of Solomon"[1], entitled "Ancient Fragment of the Key of Solomon, translated

65

from the Hebrew by Eliphaz Levi; and given in his 'Philosophie Occulte' serie II, page 136.", outlines some important base theory regarding qliphothic hierarchy, as well as qabalistic theory, with some useful adjective com-mentary. Chapter 26 of "The Mystical Qabala" by Dion Fortune[2] is devoted to the subject, as is chapter 21 of Gareth Knight's "Practical Guide to Qabalistic Symbolism: Volume 1"[3].

Another noteworthy study is the essay entitled "The Qliphoth of the Qabalah" by S.L. MacGregor-Mathers, which was originally published in 1900 as an instructional paper to initiates of the Isis-Urania temple of the Golden Dawn[4]. Another short qliphothic essay is Aleister Crowley's "Liber Arcanorum TWV ATU TOU Tahuti Quas Vidit Asar In Amennti, Sub Figura CCXXXI; Liber Carcerorum TWV Qliphoth Cum Suis Geniis, Adduntur Sigilla Et Nomina Eorum", which was originally published in "The Equinox, Volume 1, #7"[5], and re-published in "Gems From the Equinox"[6] and "The Holy Books of Thelema"[7].

The qabalistic writings of Charles Stanfield Jones[8], specifically, "Anatomy of the Body of God"[9] and "Q.B.L. or the Brides Reception"[10] suggest some rather innovative theory on pertinent subject matter. Additionally, several of Kenneth Grant's book, specifically "Nightside of Eden,"[11] "Cults of the Shadows," [12] "Outside the Circles of Time," [13] and "Hecate's Fountain,"[14] offer a valuable magickal perspective on various qliphothic topics by a truly gifted modern occult scholar. All of the above titles are highly recommended reading by the author.

Before proceeding, the following quotes are on the qliphoth, mostly by various authors known to be highly insightful on the subject of ritual magick, rather than rigid religious scholars. This does not detract from the fact that they were all known and competent qabalists. Rather, their interest of the subject sprang from especially esoteric backgrounds. The last quote is actually from a traditional qabalistic text, however the context as stated in the first sentence, qualifies it for use here.

From "The Golden Dawn: An Account of the Teachings, Rites and Ceremonies of the Golden Dawn: Book 1" edited by Israel Regardie, (c.1937): The Qlippoth are the Evil Demons of Matter and the Shells of the Dead.

From: "The Mystical Qabala" by Dion Fortune (c.1935), chapter 7: 31. ... The sphere of Malkuth abuts upon the Hells of the Averse Sephiroth, the Qliphoth, or evil demons. It is the firnament whereby Elohim separated the supernal waters of Binah from the infernal waters of Leviathan. 33. The Qliphoth (singular Qliphah, an immodest woman or harlot) are the Evil or Averse Sephiroth, each with an emanation of unbalanced force from its corresponding Sphere upon the Holy Tree; these emanations took place during the critical periods of evolution when the Sephiroth were not in equilibrium. For this reason they are referred to as the Kings of Unbalanced Force, the Kings of Edom "who ruled before there was a king in Israel", as the Bible puts it; and in the words of 'Siphrah Dzenioutha, the 'Book of Concealed Mystery' (Mathers' translation), "For before there was equilibrium, countenance beheld not countenance. And the kings of ancient time were dead, and the crowns were found no more; and the earth was desolate."

From "An Introduction to Kabalah" by W. Wynn Westcott (c.1910), page 50: The Fourth world of Assiah is filled with the lowest beings, the Evil Demons, Kliphoth or Qliphoth, the 'cortices' or shells, and with all so-called material objects, and to this world belong men, the Egos or Souls imprisoned in earthly bodies. The world also has its ten grades, each one more far from the higher forces, each one more dark and impure. First come טהו, Tohu, the Formless; and בהו, Bohu, the Void, thirdly חשך, Chesek, the Darkness, of the early universe, and from these our world was developed and now exists; then come seven hells, whose dwellers are evil beings representing all human sins; their rulers are Samael, or Satan the angel of death, and Lilith, the Asheth Zenunim, the Woman of whoredom, and this pair of demons are also called "The Beast", see Zohar ii, 255; Samael had also an incommunicable name, which was IHVH reversed; for 'Demon est Deus inversus'.[15]

From the introduction of S.L. MacGregor-Mather's "The Kabbalah Unveiled" (c.1888), page 30: The Demons are the grossest and most deficient of all forms. Their ten degrees answer to the decad of the Sephiroth, but in inverse ratio, as darkness and impurity increase with the descent of each degree. The first two are nothing but an absence of visible form and organization. The third is the abode of darkness. Next follow seven Hells occupied by those demons which represent incarnate human vices, and torture those who have given themselves up to such vices in earth-life. Their prince is 'Samael', סמאל, the angel of poison and death. His wife is the harlot, or woman of whoredom, אשת זנונים, 'Isheth Zenunim'; and united they are called the beast, חיוא, 'Chioa'. Thus the infernal trinity is completed, which is, so to speak, the averse and caricature of the supernal Creative One. Samael is considered to be identical with Satan.

From "Qabbalah: The Philosophical Writings of Solomon Ben Yehudah Ibn Gebirol", translation by Isaac Meyer (c.1888), chapter 6: If we look at the principles of this metaphysical religious philosophy in one of its simplest forms, we shall see that in each of all the objects of nature, the Qabbalists recognize two distinct elements; one is the interior, incorruptible and life-giving principle, which reveals itself in the spiritual, e.g., in vital energy or the Form; the other, is the purely exterior, plastic and material, which is considered as inert and without life or vitality, always tending to dissolution and a return to its original atoms. These two are considering as existing, in all the created, in a greater or lesser degree. The first as a symbol of Blessing and life, the latter as a symbol of Curse and death. The first, is the Qabbalistic hierarchy of the angelic host and good spirits, the latter, that of the demons or "K'lippoth", i.e., shells and evil spirits. The Deity has created both the good and the evil, and one is absolutely necessary to the existence of the other (Isa. xlv, 7).

Other than philosophical banter, little could be added here that would elaborate on the subject, in regards to generally known information. For this reason, the remainder of the chapter will be devoted to the qliphothic hierarchy. However, the student is encouraged to study any and all theory available to them regarding the qliphoth, such as those references mentioned earlier.

Here it should be reiterated that some of the theory outlined in the following pages does stray from traditional belief. Since virtually no practical qliphothic matter was derivative of ancient qabalistic texts, all available information on the subject has been deduced by various writers through their own personal studies and outlooks. In some cases, the author deems fit to slightly alter known subject matter for the benefit of the student, in the hopes that the more abstract theory will be understood by the novice. Other changes have been made where the traditional correspondences appear to be mistaken or inappropriately vague. Additionally, much original theory is also included, which have been developed through a long term study of the subject.

First, the student should be aware of some base qliphothic theory. The numerical value of קליפות is 626, and the Hebrew word "qliphoth" translated means literally "shells". In comparison to its counterpart "qabala", which translated literally means "to receive". In contrast, the two seem to differ greatly in meaning, except in the following context.

"To receive" suggests a great gift of some substance, whereas a "shell" would be a deception of substance. The shell itself giving the illusion of substance, when inside it is actually empty, meaning "to receive nothing", a "false gift", or "to deceive".

In chapter 19 of Arthur E. Powell's "The Astral Body"[16], on human astral entities, he describes "The Shell" as being:

> ...a man's astral corpse in the later stages of its disintegration, every particle of mind having left it. It is consequently without any sort of consciousness or intelligence, and drifts passively about upon astral currents. Even yet it may be galvanized for a few moments into a ghastly

burlesque of life if it happens to come within reach of a medium's aura. Under such circumstance it will still exactly resemble its departed personality in appearance and may even reproduce to some extent his familiar expressions or handwriting.

It has also the quality of being still blindly responsive to such vibrations, usually of the lowest order, as were frequently set up in it during its last stage of existence as a shade.[17]

Powell goes on to describe "The Vitalized Shell":

This entity is not, strictly speaking, human; nevertheless, it is classified here because of its outer vesture, the passive, senseless shell, was once an appendage of humanity. Such life, intelligence, desire, and will as it may possess are those of the artificial elemental animating it, this elemental being itself a creation of man's evil thought.

A vitalized shell is always malevolent: it is a true tempting demon, whose evil influence is limited only by the extent of its power. Like the shade, it is frequently used in Voodoo and Obeah forms of magic.

Moving onward, the numerical value of "the world of shells" or עולמ הקליפות is 777, and this is also the mystic number of the "Great Work"[18].

As to the structure of the "Tree of Death" glyph, its formation corresponds to that of the "Tree of Life", and it is rarely speculated on by qabalists. Several of the quotes presented earlier described the qliphoth as being lower, beneath the sphere of Malkuth. In various writings, Kenneth Grant describes it as existing on the inverse side of the spheres of the "Tree of Life", which is well taken as an innovative modern theory on the subject.

For simplicity's sake, however, the student is encouraged to consider the "Tree of Death" as being a separate and individual glyph, composed of similar attributes as possessed by the qabalistic "Tree".

The corresponding or opposing equivalents to the "Three Veils of Negative Existence"[19] on the qliphothic tree are, as described by W. Wynn Westcott, Tohu, the formless, Bohu, the void, and Chashek, the darkness. These veils are also represented by what are known as the three evil forms before Satan, and these are depicted at the top of diagram #7. The first form is Qemetiel or "Crowd of Gods", the second is Belia'al or "Worthlessness", and the third is A'athiel or "Uncertainty". These three forms give way to the actual "tree", which is described as ten hells in seven palaces, enclosed in four circles.

The four circles are representative of the four worlds which relate to the "Tree of Life". The first qabalistic world of Atziluth, the archetypal "world of emanations", corresponds to Mi Habekiyeh (מי הבכייה - 102) or "waters of weeping". The second of Briah, the "world of creation", corresponds to Mi Ha'ash (מי העש - 425) or "waters of creation". The third world of Yetzirah, the "world of formation", corresponds to Mi Auquinos (מי אוקינוס - 283) or "waters of Oceanus". Lastly, the fourth world of Assiah, the "world of manifestation" corresponds to Marmeh Im (מרמה ימ - 335) or the "False Sea". The significances of each pair parallel, yet oppose each other in various manners. They could be said to possess similar attributes, and at this point, we should leave it at that.

The uppermost aspect of the "Tree" is Shahul, the hell of the Supernals, or the Triple Hell.[20] The two kings jointly reigning over the first hell are Satan and Moloch. The third aspect of the unholy trinity is frequently misinterpreted as Lilith, the demon Queen of the ninth Hell. The correct interpretation is that the third member of the unholy trinity is the "devil".[21] Satan and Moloch are both "devils" respectively, but the true and only unnameable "devil" does not have a common name, as is the case with its counterpart, the one and only God, who heads the "Tree of Life". His incommunicable name is identical to that of the unnameable God, except in reverse, hence HVHY (הוהי). Satan and Moloch both sit on the opposing shoulders of the "devil", constantly bickering and battling with one another.

Satan is a fallen angel, the prince of evil and the enemy of God. He is frequently equated with Samael (סמאל - 131), which is a mistaken assumption, based on biblical misinterpretation. Samael may be associated with Azrael, the angel of death; but most appropriately, is designated as an angel of severity, the Archangel of Geburah in the world of Briah. Samael is not a demon, nor a fallen angel.

Moloch is also a fallen angel, and the Canaanite God of fire, to whom children were sacrificed in ancient times.

The second hell of Shahul[22] is ruled over by Beelzebub, the "Commander in Chief" of all demons, also known as the Lord of chaos and Lord of the flies.[23]

The demon king of the third hell of Supernals[24] is Lucifuge Rofacale, whose evocation is detailed in the controversial "Grand Grimoire"[25], which was unquestionably based on either "The Key of Solomon", or a variation known as "The Grand Key" or "The True Clavicles"[26]. This demon is the prime minister of the infernal regions. He is mistakenly equated with

70

Lucifer, the herald star, another fallen angel; as well, he is sometimes mistakenly equated with Focalor, the Goetic demon #41. He is properly associated with Belial, Goetic demon #68, who was created next after Lucifer, and "who entered a certain image...", as will be mentioned in chapter 5. The Solomonic equivalent of Lucifuge, who is actually Furcas, Goetic demon #50, then assumed Belial's position as king of the third hell.[27]

The fourth hell, or Abaddon[28], is ruled over by Astaroth, the Goetic demon #29. This demon was apparently depicted as a Duke at the time of the "Goetia's" writing, but has since attained the title of King, advancing greatly in office. Astaroth is also properly equated with Astarte, a fallen angel.

The demon king of Tythihoz, the fifth hell[29], is Asmodeus, the Goetic demon #32. He is often mistakenly depicted as being the son of Samael, when actually he is Samael the black, who should also not be confused with the angel Samael, discussed earlier.

The sixth hell, or Baraschechath[30], is governed by Belphegor, the Lord of opening. This demon is properly equated with Goetic demon #9, Paimon, and they are virtually identical in both office and appearance.

The demon king of Tzalemoth, the seventh hell[31], is Bael, the Goetic demon #1. He is sometimes mistakenly equated with Belphegor.

The eighth hell, or Sha'arimrath[32] is ruled over by Adramelech, the King of fire. This demon is properly associated with the Goetic demon #13, Beleth, although descriptions differ in various texts.

The demon queens of the ninth and tenth hells, collectively known as Giyehanim[33], are Lilith and Nahema. Lilith was the first woman before Eve, who later became the bride of Satan, and the demoness of debauchery. She is equated with a large variety of female demons, and is also the mother of many demons. Nahema is the Demoness of impurity, and the mortal mother of the demon king Asmodeus, whose father was Ashamdon, a Yezidic Archangel.

Each of these demon kings and Lilith rule over specific orders of demons, the hierarchy of which are illustrated in chart #15. The five accursed nations representing the tenth hell appear to correspond with the enemies of the Israelites in the "Old Testament".

The paths of the qliphoth are depicted in diagram #8. As with the qabalistic "Tree of Life", the ten primary aspects of the tree are described as the first ten paths, which correspond to the planetary hierarchy, as well as to ten of the tarot trumps, as illustrated in chart #16. The twelve secondary aspects or paths correspond to the signs of the zodiac, as well as to the remaining twelve tarot trumps, also illustrated.

Each of the qliphothic paths relate to the planetary and astrological attributes in a similar manner as the qabalistic paths, and the corresponding sigils are use to represent the significant attributes of the qliphothic aspects. Additionally, each of the tarot trumps are symbolically representative of the individual qliphothic aspects, in a fashion comparable to that of the qabalistic aspects. The tarot "Atu's" are not only keys to the mysteries of the qabala, as earlier mentioned, but also to those of the qliphoth. These mysteries are not describable through written or verbal communication, however they may be experienced personally and individually.

To begin the process of using the tarot as keys to unlock the mysteries of the qabalistic paths, one would begin by active contemplation of the individual cards. If the student has completed the exercises described in chapter 18 on the tarot in the previous volume, they would have already unknowingly initiated the process.

One should begin with the tarot trump, "The Universe", and study its image intensely. Then place yourself "in" the card. This may be accomplished by closing your eyes and mentally projecting the image into the space before you. Practice this until you create a suitable astral picture of the card's depiction. At that point, you would astrally enter the image, studying and observing every detail. This scene should live and breathe, extending in all directions as an actual landscape. The student should note any and all thoughts, feelings, reflections, revelations and experiences, fully recording everything in their tarot notebook after the experiment is completed.[34] This exercise should be performed with every tarot card, the minor arcana as well as the major, and all records should be kept in full detail.

Before proceeding in this manner to examine the qliphothic aspects of the tarot, one should have performed this exercise with each tarot card several times.

This exercise is suitable to explore the qliphothic aspects in exactly the same manner, except one should proceed by projecting the image in reverse and inverted. The coloring should be black with gray background, as if one was examining photographic negatives of the cards. Additionally, these images should be astrally entered into through the reverse of the scene, as if one was entering the "back" of the card. As before, all subsequent experiences should be duly recorded.

It should take many months, and possibly years to complete these exercises with all seventy eight tarot cards, however the student should perform no more than one of these experiments per day. The use of various decks with different designs would also prove beneficial, although the Aleister Crowley "Thoth" deck and the standard Rider-Waite deck would be the most significant for the ritual magician to utilize.

To conclude this chapter, it should be reiterated that the qliphoth is every bit as an integral part of the natural universe as is the qabala. It is a general lack of knowledge and understanding of its aspects which promotes the fear and loathing many practitioners propagate for the "world of Shells".

Would these same individuals discourage the use of the Tarot due to its negative aspects, such as the trump cards "death" and "the blasted tower"? Perhaps they would simply suggest the omission of the negative portions; to do so would compromise the integrity of the system as a whole, rendering it useless. The same could be said of the qabalistic system; that is, to omit the qliphothic aspects would render the system ineffectual and stagnant. The qliphoth is dependant on the qabala, and vice versa. This fact is an essential law of nature, as well as of magick.

DIAGRAM #7

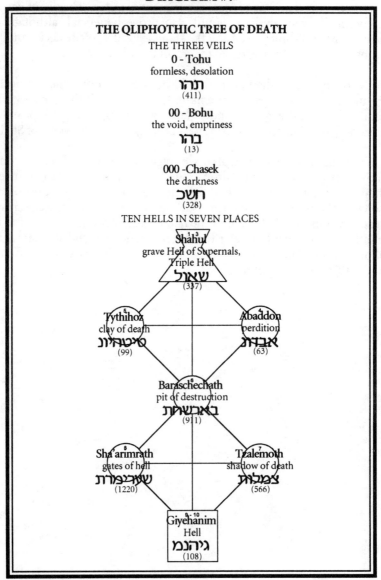

DIAGRAM #8

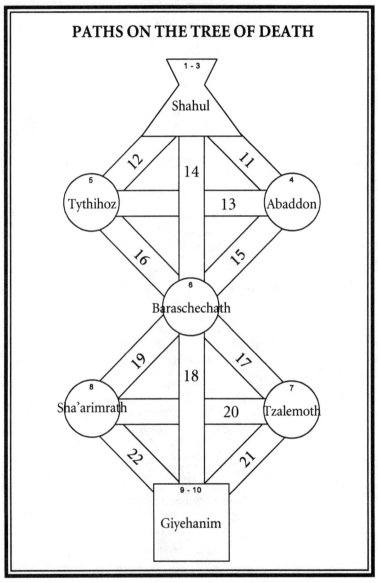

PATHS ON THE TREE OF DEATH

1 - 3

Shahul

12

14

11

5
Tythihoz

13

4
Abaddon

16

15

6
Baraschechath

19

18

17

8
Sha'arimrath

20

7
Tzalemoth

22

21

9 - 10

Giyehanim

CHART #15-A

ORDERS OF DEMONS

0 - Qemetiel
Crown of Gods, First Devil
קמטיאל
(190)

00 - Belia'al
Worthlessness, Wickedness
בליעל
(142)

000 -A'athiel
Uncertainty
עתיאל
(511)

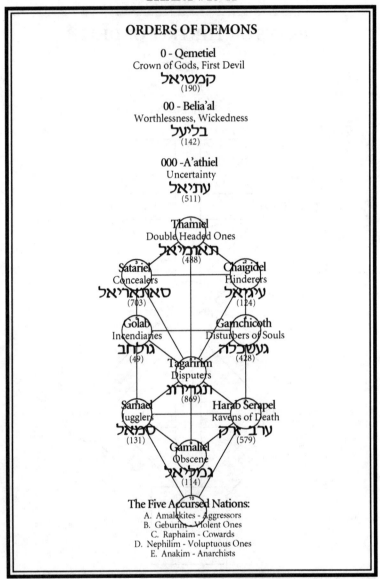

Thamiel
Double Headed Ones
תאומיאל
(488)

Satariel
Concealers
סאתאריאל
(703)

Chaigidel
Hinderers
עיגיאל
(124)

Golab
Incendiaries
גולחב
(49)

Gamchicoth
Disturbers of Souls
געשכלה
(428)

Tagaririm
Disputers
תגרירת
(869)

Samael
Jugglers
סמאל
(131)

Harab Serapel
Ravens of Death
ערב אֶרָק
(579)

Gamaliel
Obscene
גמליאל
(114)

The Five Accursed Nations:
A. Amalekites - Aggressors
B. Geburim - Violent Ones
C. Raphaim - Cowards
D. Nephilim - Voluptuous Ones
E. Anakim - Anarchists

76

CHART #15-B

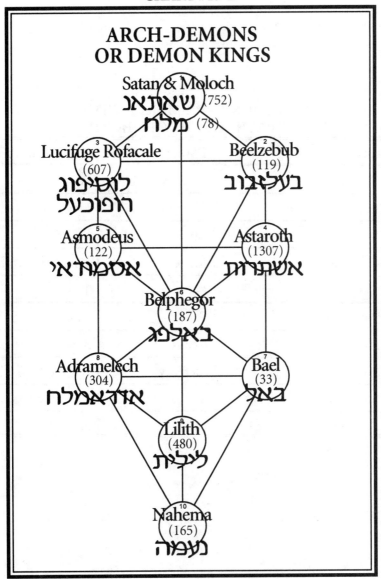

ARCH-DEMONS
OR DEMON KINGS

Satan & Moloch
שאתאנ (752)
מלח (78)

Lucifuge Rofacale
(607)
לוסיפוג
רופוכעל

Beelzebub
(119)
בעלזבוב

Asmodeus
(122)
אסמודאי

Astaroth
(1307)
אשתרות

Belphegor
(187)
באלפג

Adramelech
(304)
אודאאמלח

Bael
(33)
באל

Lilith
(480)
לילת

Nahema
(165)
נעמה

CHART #16-A - PRIMARY ASPECTS
22 PATHS OF THE QLIPHOTH

Path	Planet	Tarot Trump
1. Thamiel	Primum Mobile	Fool
2. Chaigidel	Fixed planets	Magician
3. Sateriel	Saturn	Universe
4. Gamchicoth	Jupiter	Wheel of Fortune
5. Golab	Mars	Tower
6. Tagaririm	Sun	Sun
7. Harab Serapel	Venus	Aeon
8. Samael	Mercury	Hanged Man
9. Gamaliel	Moon	High Priestess
10. Five Accursed Nations	Earth	Empress

CHART #16-B - SECONDARY ASPECTS
22 PATHS OF THE QLIPHOTH

Path	Sign	Tarot Trump
11. Ba'airiron (בעירירון - 548) The Flock	Aries	Emporer
12. Adimiron (אדימירון - 321) Bloody	Taurus	Hierophant
13. Tzalalimiron (צללד מירון - 460) Clangers	Gemini	Lovers
14. Shichiriron (שיחרירון - 784) Black	Cancer	Chariot
15. Shalehbiron (שלהבירון - 603) Flaming	Leo	Strength
16. Tzaphiriron (צפרירון - 636) Scratchers	Virgo	Hermit
17. A'abiriron (עבירירון - 548) Clayey	Libra	Justice
18. Necheshthiron (נחשתירון - 1024) Brazen	Scorpio	Death
19. Necheshiron (נחשירון - 624) Snakey	Sagittarius	Temperance
20. Dagdagiron (דגדגירון - 280) Fishy	Capricorn	Devil
21. Bahimiron (בהימירון - 323) Bestial	Aquarius	Star
22. Nashimiron (נשימירון - 666) Malignant Women	Pisces	Moon

5

THE GOETIC DEMONS

Within the pages of the "Goetia" is recorded the names, orders and offices of seventy two demons or evil spirits. These are listed in a numerical order in the first section, under the subtitle "שמ המפורש"[1]. This cohort of demons, plus all of their legions was said to have totaled over seven million, at the time of the "Goetia's" writing. The populous is likely to have increased over the centuries, however this is strictly conjecture, and need not be discussed at this point. There are numerous charts in this chapter which efficiently define specific attributes of each individual spirit. These have all been based on the given information, presumably accurate at the time of writing. It should be expected that in the thirty centuries that have passed, some changes have taken place, and the author is aware of several. However, the sources of this information were of a somewhat questionable nature, and no published evidence exists to support these claims. Therefore, we shall adhere to the subject matter offered in the translated text.

As for the legend of the spirits themselves, a paragraph in the text, immediately following their descriptions, sheds a narrow ray of light in regards to their existence:

> These be the 72 mighty Kings and Princes which King Solomon commanded into a vessel of brass, together with their legions, of whom BELIAL, BILETH, ASMODAY and GAAP were chief. And it is to be noted that Solomon did this because of their pride, for he never declared other reason why he thus bound them. And when he had thus bound them up and sealed the vessel, he by Divine Power did chase them all into a deep lake or hole in Babylon. And they of Babylon, wondering to see such a thing, they did then go wholly into the lake, to break the vessel open, expecting to find great store of treasure therein. But when they had broken it open, out flew the chief spirits immediately, with their legions following them; and they were all restored to their former places except BELIAL, who entered into a certain image, and thence gave answers unto those who did offer sacrifices unto him, and did worship the image as their God, etc.[2]

The individual spirits correspond to various aspects of the qliphoth, in a manner similar to how the biblical angels relate to the qabala. Their particular order was represented by a title or rank, either king, prince, duke, knight, earl, marquis, president (or prelate). These each fall under a specific planetary influence[3], which determines their corresponding qliphothic orders, as depicted in chart #17.[4]

This chart includes the respective number designated to each spirit, which are determined in the text translation, as well as the proper Hebrew spellings of each name, and the appropriate English pronunciation thereof.[5] Also depicted in chart #17 are the numerical value of each name, the titles of the individual demons, and the astrological decanates over which each rules, or holds dominion. It has been suggested that these spirits may only be called during the period of their ruling decanate; however this assumption is incorrect, as these individuals may be summoned at any time, so long as the criteria outlined in the next chapter are adhered to.

Chart #18 illustrates the planetary hierarchies of the respective demonic orders, according to the number of legions controlled by each, as determined in the text translation of the "Goetia".[6]

Chart #19 separates the demons by their Goetic titles and planetary attributions, in a numerical order. The individuals with asterisks next to their names indicate that the title noted in that particular column is a secondary or lesser title than their primary. For example, Gaap holds a primary title of prince, as well as a secondary title of president. Eight of these spirits were said to have held two titles, at the time of the "Goetia's" writing.

Charts #20-25 divide the seventy-two demons into their respective categories as ruling ascendent, succedent or cadent decanates, by either day or night. These have been numbered according to their corresponding qliphothic paths. The numbers in parentheses are the spirit's numerical designations, as determined by the text translation. Also noted in parentheses are the demons titles and ruling planetary influences. The recorded magickal images, or general appearance, of each demon is additionally given in these six charts.

Chart #26 lists each of the demon's "offices" or specific magickal talents. These offices generally correlate to the known attributes of the spirit's governing planetary aspects.

Chart #27 depicts each of the demon's representative sigils, which are specifically used to evoke and control them individually. Eight of these include two sigils attributed to one demon, which have been derived from the various manuscripts available to the translator, S.L. MacGregor-Mathers. In these cases, either sigil should prove effective.

There is not much which could be added here that would elaborate on the known data concerning these spirits of the "Lesser Key of Solomon", in lieu of the author taking certain liberties by expounding on his personal knowledge. However, much of this information was derived through rather questionable means, and no hard evidence exists to substantiate his claims. Therefore, we will end this chapter here, and continue on to the preparations for actual "Goetic" evocation.

Chart #17 - GOETIC DEMONS

English	Hebrew	Value	Title		Sign
1. Bael	באל	33	King	Day Demon	Ascendant	Aries
2. Agares	אגאר	205	Duke	Day Demon	Succedent	Aries
3. Vassago	ושאגו	316	Prince	Day Demon	Cadent	Aries
4. Gamigin	גאמיגין	117	Marquis	Day Demon	Ascendant	Taurus
5. Marbas	מארבאש	544	President	Day Demon	Succedent	Taurus
6. Valefor	ואלפר	317	Duke	Day Demon	Cadent	Taurus
7. Amon	אמון	97	Marquis	Day Demon	Ascendant	Gemini
8. Barbatos	בארבטוש	519	Duke	Day Demon	Succedent	Gemini
9. Paimon	פאימון	187	King	Day Demon	Cadent	Gemini
10. Buer	בואר	209	President	Day Demon	Ascendant	Cancer
11. Gusion	גוסיון	135	Duke	Day Demon	Succedent	Cancer
12. Sitri	שיטרי	529	Prince	Day Demon	Cadent	Cancer
13. Beleth	בלאת	433	King	Day Demon	Ascendant	Leo

14. Leraikhe	ליראיכה	266	Marquis	Day Demon	Succedent	Leo
15. Eligos	אליגוס	350	Duke	Day Demon	Cadent	Leo
16. Zepar	זאפר	371	Duke	Day Demon	Ascendant	Virgo
17. Botis	בוטיס	327	President/Earl	Day Demon	Succedent	Virgo
18. Bathin	באתין	463	Duke	Day Demon	Cadent	Virgo
19. Sallos	שאלוס	637	Duke	Day Demon	Ascendant	Libra
20. Purson	פורסון	642	King	Day Demon	Succedent	Libra
21. Marax	מאראקס	332	President/Earl	Day Demon	Cadent	Libra
22. Ipos	יפוס	396	Prince/Earl	Day Demon	Ascendant	Scorpio
23. Aim	אים	51	Duke	Day Demon	Succedent	Scorpio
24. Naberius	נבריוס	552	Marquis	Day Demon	Cadent	Scorpio
25. Glasya-Labolas	גלאסיאלבולס	462	President/Earl	Day Demon	Ascendant	Sagittarius
26. Bim	בים	52	Duke	Day Demon	Succedent	Sagittarius
27. Ronove	רונוב	272	Marquis/Earl	Day Demon	Cadent	Sagittarius
28. Berith	בריתה	612	Duke	Day Demon	Ascendant	Capricorn

Name	Hebrew	Number	Rank		Dignity	Zodiac
29. Astaroth	אשתרות	1307	Duke	Day Demon	Succedent	Capricorn
30. Furneus	פורנאש	637	Marquis	Day Demon	Cadent	Capricorn
31. Foras	פוראש	587	President	Day Demon	Ascendant	Aquarius
32. Asmodeus	אשמודאי	122	King	Day Demon	Succedent	Aquarius
33. Gaap	גאפ	153	President	Day Demon	Cadent	Aquarius
34. Furfur	פורפור	572	Earl	Day Demon	Ascendant	Pisces
35. Marchosias	מרחוש	554	Marquis	Day Demon	Succedent	Pisces
36. Stolas	שטולוש	651	Prince	Day Demon	Cadent	Pisces
37. Phenex	פנאג	221	Marquis	Night Demon	Ascendant	Aries
38. Halphas	האלפש	416	Earl	Night Demon	Succedent	Aries
39. Malphas	מאלפש	451	President	Night Demon	Cadent	Aries
40. Raum	ראום	247	Earl	Night Demon	Ascendant	Taurus
41. Focalor	פוכלור	342	Duke	Night Demon	Succedent	Taurus
42. Vepar	וגאר	287	Duke	Night Demon	Cadent	Taurus
43. Sabnock	שבנכ	382	Marquis	Night Demon	Ascendant	Gemini

	Hebrew	Number	Rank		Dignity	Sign
44. Shax	שע	390	Marquis	Night Demon	Succedent	Gemini
45. Vine	וינא	67	King/Duke	Night Demon	Cadent	Gemini
46. Bifrous	ביפר	298	Earl	Night Demon	Ascendant	Cancer
47. Uval	אואל	38	Duke	Night Demon	Succedent	Cancer
48. Haagenti	האגנתי	538	President	Night Demon	Cadent	Cancer
49. Crocell	כרוכל	276	Duke	Night Demon	Ascendant	Leo
50. Furcas	פורכאש	607	Knight	Night Demon	Succedent	Leo
51. Balaam	באלעם	143	King	Night Demon	Cadent	Leo
52. Alloces	אלוך	57	Duke	Night Demon	Ascendant	Virgo
53. Caim	כאים	71	President	Night Demon	Succedent	Virgo
54. Murmur	מורמור	492	Duke/Earl	Night Demon	Cadent	Virgo
55. Orobas	אורואבש	516	Prince	Night Demon	Ascendant	Libra
56. Gamori	גמורי	259	Duke	Night Demon	Succedent	Libra
57. Oso	ושו	312	President	Night Demon	Cadent	Libra
58. Avnas	אונס	357	President	Night Demon	Ascendant	Scorpio

Name	Hebrew	No.	Rank	Demon	House	Sign
59. Oriax	וריאן	307	Marquis	Night Demon	Succedent	Scorpio
60. Naphula	נפולא	167	Duke	Night Demon	Cadent	Scorpio
61. Zagan	זאגן	61	King/President	Night Demon	Ascendant	Sagittarius
62. Volac	ואלכ	57	President	Night Demon	Succedent	Sagittarius
63. Andras	אנדרוש	555	Marquis	Night Demon	Cadent	Sagittarius
64. Havres	האור	212	Duke	Night Demon	Ascendant	Capricorn
65. Andrealphus	אנדראלפוס	666	Marquis	Night Demon	Succedent	Capricorn
66. Kimaris	כימריש	277	Marquis	Night Demon	Cadent	Capricorn
67. Amdukias	אמדוך	71	Duke	Night Demon	Ascendant	Aquarius
68. Belial	בליאל	73	King	Night Demon	Succedent	Aquarius
69. Decarabia	דקראבא	234	Marquis	Night Demon	Cadent	Aquarius
70. Seere	שאר	501	Prince	Night Demon	Ascendant	Pisces
71. Dantalion	דנטליון	550	Duke	Night Demon	Succedent	Pisces
72. Andromalius	אנדרומליאל	332	Earl	Night Demon	Cadent	Pisces

CHART #18-A

SOLAR DEMON HIERARCHY (KINGS) Qliphoth Order of Thagirion		
#	Demon	Legions
1	9. Paimon	(200)
2	13. Beleth	(85)
3	32. Asmoday	(72)
4	1. Bael	(66)
5	68. Belial	(50)
6	51. Balaam	(40)
7	45. Vine	(36)
8	61. Zagan	(33)
9	20. Purson	(22)

CHART #18-B

SATURNIAN DEMON HIERARCHY (KNIGHT) Qliphoth Order of Satariel		
#	Demon	Legions
1	50. Furcas	(20)

CHART #18-C

JUPITERIAN DEMON HIERARCHY (PRINCES) Qliphoth Order of Gha'agsheblah		
#	Demon	Legions
1	33. Gaap	(66)
2	12. Sitri	(60)
3	22. Ipos	(36)
4	3. Vassago 36. Stolas 70. Seere	(26) (26) (26)
5	55. Orobas	(20)

CHART #18-D

MARTIAN DEMON HIERARCHY (EARLS) Qliphoth Order of Golachab		
#	Demon	Legions
1	17. Botis 46. Bifrous	(60) (60)
2	22. Ipos 25. Glasya-Labolas 45. Vine 72. Andromalius	(36) (36) (36) (36)
3	21. Marax 40. Raum 54. Murmur	(30) (30) (30)
4	34. Furfur 38. Halphas	(26) (26)
5	27. Ronove	(19)

CHART #18-E

CHART #18-F

VENUTIAN DEMON HIERARCHY (DUKES) Qliphoth Order of A'arab Zaraq		
#	Demon	Legions
1	15. Eligos	(60)
2	49. Crocell	(48)
3	11. Gusion 29. Astaroth	(40) (40)
4	47. Uval	(37)
5	52. Alloces 60. Naphula 64. Havres 71. Dantalion	(36) (36) (36) (36)
6	2. Agares	(31)
7	8. Barbatos 18. Bathin 19. Sallos 26. Bim 41. Focalor 54. Murmur	(30) (30) (30) (30) (30) (30)
8	42. Vepar 67. Amdukias	(29) (29)
9	16. Zepar 23. Aim 28. Berith 56. Gamori	(26) (26) (26) (26)
10	6. Valefor	(10)

MERCURIAL DEMON HIEARCHY (PRESIDENTS) Qliphoth Order of Samael		
#	Demon	Legions
1	33. Gaap	(66)
2	17. Botis	(60)
3	10. Buer	(50)
4	39. Malphas	(40)
5	62. Volac	(38)
6	5. Marbas 25. Glasya-Labolas 58. Avnas	(36) (36) (36)
7	48. Haagenti 61. Zagan	(33) (33)
8	21. Marax 53. Caim 57. Oso	(30) (30) (30)
9	31. Foras	(29)

CHART #18-G

LUNAR DEMON HIERARCHY (MARQUIS) Qliphoth Order of Gamaliel		
#	**Demon**	Legions
1	43. Sabnock	(50)
2	7. Amon	(40)
3	4. Gamigin 14. Leraikhe 35. Marchosias 44. Shax 59. Oriax 63. Andras 65. Andrealphus 69. Decarabia	(30) (30) (30) (30) (30) (30) (30)
4	30. Furneus	(29)
5	37. Phenex 66. Kimaris	(20) (20)
6	24. Naberius 27. Ronove	(19) (19)

CHART #19 - GOETIC TITLES AND PLANETARY ATTRIBUTIONS (* - denotes secondary title.)

King Solar	Duke Venus	Prince Jupiter	Marquis Lunar	President Mercury	Earl Mars	Knight Saturn
1. Bael	2. Agares / 47. Uval	3. Vassago	4. Gamigin	5. Marbas	17. Botis*	50. Furcas
9. Paimon	6. Valefor / 69. Decarabia	12. Sitri	7. Amon	10. Buer	21. Marax*	
13. Beleth	8. Barbatos / 49. Crocell	22. Ipos	14. Leraikhe	17. Botis	22. Ipos*	
20. Purson	11. Gusion / 52. Alloces	33. Gaap	24. Naberius	21. Marax	25. Glasya-Labolas*	
32. Asmoday	15. Eligos / 54. Murmur	36. Stolas	27. Ronove	25. Glasya-Labolas	27. Ronove*	
45. Vine	16. Zepar / 56. Gamori	55. Orobas	30. Furneus	31. Foras	34. Furfur	
51. Balaam	18. Bathin / 60. Naphula	70. Seere	35. Marchosias	33. Gaap*	38. Halphas	
61. Zagan	19. Sallos / 64. Havres		37. Phenex	39. Malphas	40. Raum	
68. Belial	23. Aim / 67. Amdukias		43. Sabnock	48. Haagenti	45. Vine*	
	26. Bim / 71. Dantalion		44. Shax	53. Caim	46. Bifrous	
	28. Berith		59. Oriax	57. Oso	54. Murmur	
	29. Astaroth		63. Andras	58. Avnas	72. Andromalius	
	41. Focalor		65. Andrealphus	61. Zagan*		
	42. Vepar		66. Kimaris	62. Volac		

92

CHART #20

Demons (ascendant - by day)	Magical Images
11. (1) Bael (King - Solar)	Shape-shifting, cat, toad, man.
12. (4) Gamigin (Marquis - Lunar)	Small Horse or ass, hoarse voice.
13. (7) Amon (Marquis - Lunar)	Wolf with serpent's tail, breathing fire. Changes to man with raven's head, dog's teeth.
14. (10) Buer (President - Mercury)	Sagittarian figure, centaur, archer.
15. (13) Beleth (King - Solar)	Angry man on pale horse. Strong breath. Accompanied by many musicians.
16. (16) Zepar (Duke - Venus)	Man in red armour, as a soldier.
17. (19) Sallos (Duke - Venus)	Man as a soldier, with ducal crown, riding a crocodile.
18. (22) Ipos (Prince/Earl - Jupiter/Mars)	Angel with lion's head, webbed feet, hare's tail. ("777" says horse)
19. (25) Glasya-Labolas (President/Earl - Mercury/Mars)	Dog with gryphon's wings.
20. (28) Berith (Duke - Venus)	Man as soldier dressed in red, with gold crown, riding a red horse.
21. (31) Foras (President - Mercury)	Strong man.
22. (34) Furfur (Earl - Mars)	Hart with a fiery tail, then an angel.

CHART #21

Demons (succedent - by day)	Magical Images
11. (2) Agares (Duke - Venus)	Old man riding a crocodile, carrying a goshawk on his fist.
12. (5) Marbas (President - Mercury)	Great Lion.
13. (8) Barbatos (Duke - Venus)	With 4 noble Kings & great troops.
14. (11) Gusion (Duke - Venus)	A "Xenopilus".
15. (14) Leraikhe (Marquis - Lunar)	An archer in green.
16. (17) Botis (President/Earl - Mercury/Mars)	An ugly viper, then changing to a man with great teeth & 2 horns.
17. (20) Purson (King - Solar)	Lion-faced man riding on a bear, carrying a viper. Trumpets before him.
18. (23) Aim (Duke - Venus)	Man with 3 heads, 1st a serpent's, 2nd a man's w/ 2 stars on forehead, 3rd a calf's. Rides on a viper, & carrying a firebrand.
19. (26) Bim (Duke - Venus)	Dragon with 3 heads, 1st like a dog's, 2nd a gryphons, 3rd a viper's. High voice.
20. (29) Astaroth (Duke - Venus)	Hurtful angel riding a dragon, with a viper in right hand. Strong breath.
21. (32) Asmoday (King - Solar)	3 heads, 1st a bull's, 2nd a man's, 3rd a ram's. Serpent's tail, webbed feet, riding a dragon, carrying a lance with a banner.
22. (35) Marchosias (Marquis - Lunar)	Wolf with gryphon's wings, serpent's tail, breathing fire.

CHART #22

Demons (cadent - by day)	Magical Images
11. (3) Vassago (Prince - Jupiter)	Old man riding a crocodile, carrying a goshawk on his fist.
12. (6) Valefor (Duke - Venus)	Ass's head on lion's body, bellowing.
13. (9) Paimon (King - Solar)	Crowned man riding dromedary. Many musicians accompanying.
14. (12) Sitri (Prince - Jupiter)	Leopard's head, gryphon's wings.
15. (15) Eligos (Duke - Venus)	Knight carrying a lance, banner & serpent.
16. (18) Bathin (Duke - Venus)	Man with serpent's tail, riding a pale horse.
17. (21) Marax (President/Earl - Mercury/Mars)	Bull with man's face.
18. (24) Naberius (Marquis - Lunar)	Black crane with hoarse voice.
19. (27) Ronove (Marquis/Earl - Lunar/Mars)	Monster
20. (30) Furneus (Marquis - Lunar)	Sea monster
21. (33) Gaap (President - Mercury)	Man followed by 4 Kings, as a guide.
22. (36) Stolas (Prince - Jupiter)	Raven.

CHART #23

Demons (ascendant - by night)	Magical Images
11. (37) Phenex (Marquis - Lunar)	Phoenix with child's voice.
12. (40) Raum (Earl - Mars)	Crow.
13. (43) Sabnock (Marquis - Lunar)	Armed soldier with lion's head, riding a pale horse.
14. (46) Bifrous (Earl - Mars)	Monster.
15. (49) Crocell (Duke - Venus)	Angel.
16. (52) Alloces (Duke - Venus)	Soldier with face of a red lion, flaming eyes, riding on horse.
17. (55) Orobas (Prince - Jupiter)	Horse.
18. (58) Avnas (President - Mercury)	Flaming fire, then a man.
19. (61) Zagan (King/President - Solar/Mercury)	Bull with gryphon's wings.
20. (64) Havres (Duke - Venus)	Leopard.
21. (67) Amdukias (Duke - Venus)	First a unicorn, then a man.
22. (70) Seere (Prince - Jupiter)	Beautiful man riding winged horse.

CHART #24

Demons (succendent - by night)	Magical Images
11. (38) Halphus (Earl - Mars)	Stock dove, hoarse voice.
12. (41) Focalor (Duke - Venus)	Man with gryphon's wings.
13. (44) Shax (Marquis - Lunar)	Stock dove, hoarse voice.
14. (47) Uval (Duke - Venus)	Dromedary.
15. (50) Furcas (Knight - Saturn)	Cruel old man w/long white hair & beard, riding a pale horse, carrying sharp weapons.
16. (53) Caim (President - Mercury)	First a thrush, then man w/sharp sword.
17. (56) Gamori (Duke - Venus)	Beautiful woman with a duchess crown tied at waist, riding a great camel.
18. (59) Oriax (Marquis - Lunar)	A lion with serpent's tail, riding a horse carrying hissing serpents in right hand.
19. (62) Volac (President - Mercury)	Child with angel's wings, riding a 2 headed serpent.
20. (65) Andrealphus (Marquis - Lunar)	Peacock, making great noises.
21. (68) Belial (King - Solar)	2 beautiful angels sitting in a chariot of fire.
22. (71) Dantalion (Duke - Venus)	Man with many countenances, all men's & women's, with book in right hand.

CHART #25

Demons (cadent - by night)	Magical Images
11. (39) Malphas (President - Mercury)	Crow with hoarse voice.
12. (42) Vepar (Duke - Venus)	Mermaid.
13. (45) Vine (King/Duke - Solar/Venus)	Lion riding a horse, carrying a viper.
14. (48) Haagenti (President - Mercury)	Bull with gryphon's wings.
15. (51) Balaam (King - Solar)	With 3 heads, 1st a bull's, 2nd a man's, 3rd a ram's. Flaming eyes, serpent's tail. Riding a bear, with boshawk on his fist.
16. (54) Murmur (Duke/Earl - Venus/Mars)	Warrior riding a gryphon, wearing a ducal crown, trumpeteers before him.
17. (57) Oso (President - Mercury)	Leopard.
18. (60) Naphula (Duke - Venus)	Lion with gryphon's wings.
19. (63) Andras (Marquis - Lunar)	Angel with black raven's head, riding a black wolf, carrying a sharp sword.
20. (66) Kimaris (Marquis - Lunar)	Warrior on black horse.
21. (69) Decarabia (Marquis - Lunar)	A star in a pentacle.
22. (72) Andromalius (Earl - Mars)	Man holding a great serpent.

Chart #26 - OFFICES OF THE GOETIC DEMONS

1. Bael	Makes men invisible, gives wisdom.
2. Agares	Brings back runaways, teaches all languages, destroys spiritual & temporal dignities, causes earthquakes, chases off enemies
3. Vassago	Declares things past, present & future, discovers things lost or hidden.
4. Gamigin	Teaches the liberal sciences, gives news of those who have died in sin, summons the souls of drowned men & those in purgatory.
5. Marbas	Answers questions concerning all things hidden or secret, causes & cures diseases, teaches the mechanical arts, changes men into various shapes.
6. Valefor	Teaches how to steal.
7. Amon	Declares things past and future, procures love, reconciles friends and enemies.
8. Barbatos	Teaches all sciences, reveals treasures concealed by magic, declares things past and future, reconciles friends.
9. Paimon	Teaches all arts, sciences and secrets, gives and confirms dignities, makes men subject unto the magician, provides familiars.
10. Buer	Teaches moral, natural and logical philosophy, teaches the virtues of herbs and plants, cures diseases, provides familiars.
11. Gusion	Declares things past, present and future, answers all questions, makes and reconciles friendships, gives honor and dignity.
12. Sitri	Brings love to men and women, causes nakedness.
13. Beleth	Brings love to men and women.

14. Leraikhe	Causes battles and contests, makes wounds caused by arrows to putrefy.
15. Eligos	Discovers hidden things, declares the future, declares the outcome of wars and battles, causes love.
16. Zepar	Brings women's love to men, makes women barren.
17. Botis	Declares things past and present, reconciles friends and enemies.
18. Bathin	Teaches the virtues of herbs and stones, transports men suddenly to other countries.
19. Sallos	Brings love to men and women.
20. Purson	Discovers hidden things and tresures, declares things past, present and future, answers all questions, provides familiars.
21. Marax	Teaches astronomy, liberal sciences and the virtues of herbs and stones, provides familiars.
22. Ipos	Declares things past, present and future, makes men witty and bold.
23. Aim	Makes men witty, answers questions regarding private matters.
24. Naberius	Makes men cunning in all arts and sciences, restores lost dignities and honors.
25. Glasya-Labolas	Teaches all arts and sciences, causes bloodshed and murder, declares things past, present and future, causes love of friends and enemies, makes men invisible.
26. Bim	Changes the place of the dead, causes spirits to gather around sepulchres, gives riches, makes men wise and eloquent, answers questions.
27. Ronove	Teaches the art of rhetoric and languages, provides servants, reconciles friends and enemies.

28. Berith	Declares things past, present and future, answers questions, turns metals into gold, gives and confirms dignities.
29. Astaroth	Declares things past, present and future, answers questions, discovers all secrets, teaches the liberal sciences.
30. Furneus	Teaches the art of rhetoric and languages, reconciles friends and enemies.
31. Foras	Teaches the virtues of herbs and stones, and the arts of logic and ethics, makes men invisible, gives long life, makes men eloquent, discovers treasures, recovers lost things.
32. Asmodeus	Gives the ring of virtue, teaches the arts of astronomy, arithmetic, geometry and craftsmanship, answers all questions, makes men invincible, discovers and guards treasures.
33. Gaap	Teaches philosophy and liberal sciences, makes men ignorant, causes love and hatred, teaches how to consecrate things, provides familiars, answers questions, declares things past, present and future, transports and returns men.
34. Furfur	Brings love to men and women, causes storms, lightning, thunder and winds, answers questions.
35. Marchosias	Fights, answers questions.
36. Stolas	Teaches the art of astronomy, and the virtues of herbs and stones.
37. Phenex	Teaches all sciences, answers questions.
38. Halphas	Builds towers, provides weaponry.
39. Malphas	Builds towers, tells the secrets of enemies.
40. Raum	Steals treasures, destroys cities and dignities, declares the past, present and future, reconciles friends and enemies.

41. Focalor	Drowns men, sinks ships of war, causes winds and rough seas.
42. Vepar	Guides ships of war, causes storms and calm seas, causes death by putrefying wounds or sores.
43. Sabnock	Builds towers, castles and cities, causes worms to afflict wounds and sores, provides familiars.
44. Shax	Takes away sight, hearing or understanding, steals money, transports objects, discovers hidden things, provides familiars.
45. Vine	Discovers things hidden, reveals the presence of witches and wizards, declares things past, present and future, builds towers, destroys walls, causes storms.
46. Bifrous	Teaches astrology, geometry, arts and sciences, the virtues of stones and herbs, changes the place of the dead.
47. Uval	Brings love to men, declares things past, present and future, reconciles friends and enemies.
48. Haagenti	Gives wisdom, teaches diverse subjects, turns metals into gold, turns wine into water and vice versa.
49. Crocell	Teaches mysticism, geometry and liberal sciences, produces the sound of rushing water, heats water.
50. Furcas	Teaches philosophy, astrology, rhetoric, logic, cheiromancy, and pyromancy.
51. Balaam	Declares things past, present and future, makes men invisible and witty.
52. Alloces	Teaches astronomy and liberal sciences, provides familiars.
53. Caim	Teaches the understanding of animal's voices and that of water, answers questions, declares the future.

54. Murmur	Teaches philosophy, causes the souls of the deceased to appear and answer questions.
55. Orobas	Declares things past, present and future, gives dignities and honors, reconciles friends and enemies, answers questions.
56. Gamori	Declares things past, present and future, discovers hidden treasures, brings love to men.
57. Oso	Teaches the liberal sciences, answers questions, changes men's shape.
58. Avnas	Teaches astrology and liberal sciences, provides familiars, discovers hidden treasures.
59. Oriax	Teaches the virtues of the stars and planets, transforms men, gives and confirms dignities and honors, reconciles friends and enemies.
60. Naphula	Teaches craftsmanship and manual professions, philosophy, and other sciences.
61. Zagan	Makes men witty, turns water and blood into wine and vice versa, turns metals into coins, gives wisdom.
62. Volac	Discovers hidden treasures and also serpents.
63. Andras	Sows discord, kills men.
64. Havres	Declares things past, present and future, answers questions, kills men by fire.
65. Andrealphus	Teaches geometry, measurements, and astronomy, transforms men into birds.
66. Kimaris	Teaches grammar, logic and rhetoric, discovers lost things and hidden treasures.
67. Amdukias	Makes trees bend and fall.
68. Belial	Distributes presentations and titles, reconciles friends and enemies, provides familiars.

69. Decarabia	Teaches the virtues of herbs and stones, provides birds as familiars.
70. Seere	To transport things, to deliver messages and return, discovers thefts, lost things and hidden treasures.
71. Dantalion	Teaches all arts and sciences, declares secrets, changes people's thoughts, brings love to men and women, shows a vison of the likeness of any person.
72. Andromalius	Returns stolen things, captures thieves, exposes wickedness and underhanded dealings, punishes thieves, discovers hidden treasures.

CHART #27
SIGILS OF THE GOETIC DEMONS

Follows on the next four pages...

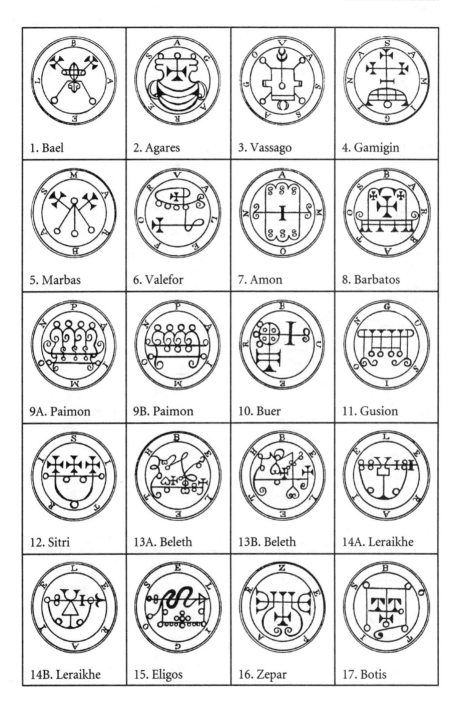

1. Bael	2. Agares	3. Vassago	4. Gamigin
5. Marbas	6. Valefor	7. Amon	8. Barbatos
9A. Paimon	9B. Paimon	10. Buer	11. Gusion
12. Sitri	13A. Beleth	13B. Beleth	14A. Leraikhe
14B. Leraikhe	15. Eligos	16. Zepar	17. Botis

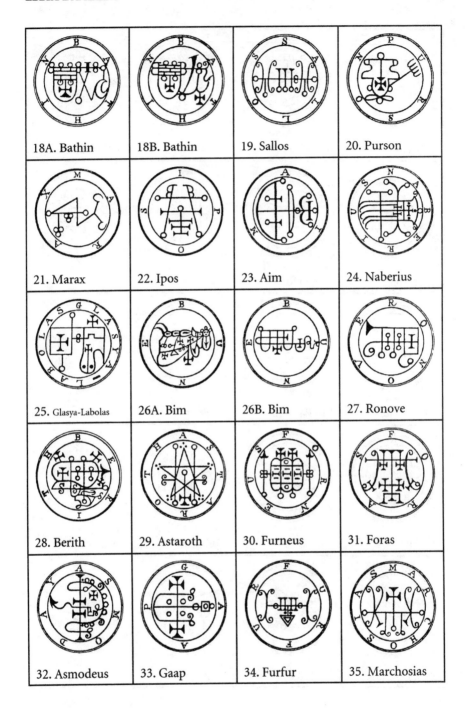

18A. Bathin	18B. Bathin	19. Sallos	20. Purson
21. Marax	22. Ipos	23. Aim	24. Naberius
25. Glasya-Labolas	26A. Bim	26B. Bim	27. Ronove
28. Berith	29. Astaroth	30. Furneus	31. Foras
32. Asmodeus	33. Gaap	34. Furfur	35. Marchosias

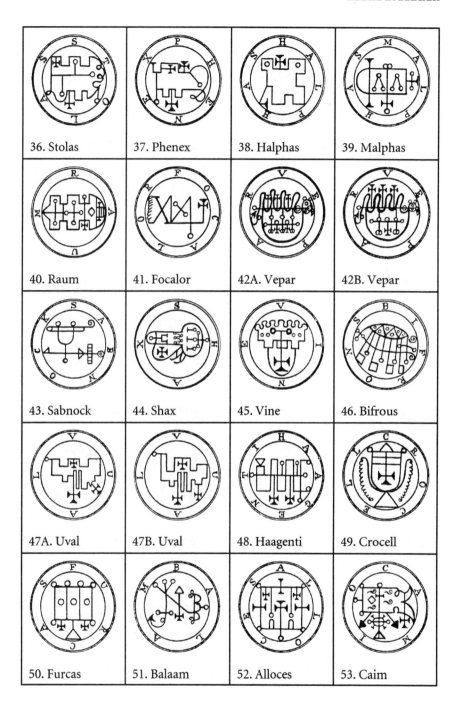

36. Stolas	37. Phenex	38. Halphas	39. Malphas
40. Raum	41. Focalor	42A. Vepar	42B. Vepar
43. Sabnock	44. Shax	45. Vine	46. Bifrous
47A. Uval	47B. Uval	48. Haagenti	49. Crocell
50. Furcas	51. Balaam	52. Alloces	53. Caim

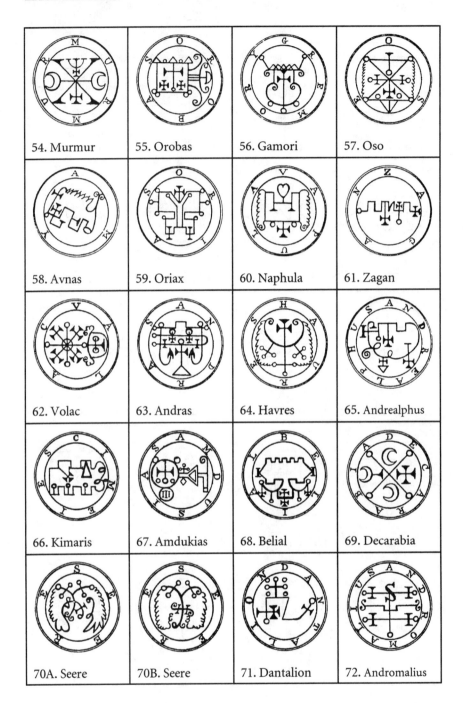

54. Murmur	55. Orobas	56. Gamori	57. Oso
58. Avnas	59. Oriax	60. Naphula	61. Zagan
62. Volac	63. Andras	64. Havres	65. Andrealphus
66. Kimaris	67. Amdukias	68. Belial	69. Decarabia
70A. Seere	70B. Seere	71. Dantalion	72. Andromalius

6

PREPARATIONS FOR GOETIC EVOCATION

A goetic evocation should only be performed for one single and definite purpose or intention, thought out and decided upon well in advance. The act is not to be attempted simply to see if it can be done. This would surely prove extremely foolish, and might easily lead to certain disaster, should the beginning or intermediate practitioner happen to succeed. The specific purpose is most appropriately to obtain certain information of an occult nature; although various others are suggested by the offices of the demons in the "Goetia" itself, such as the destruction of one's enemies, locating lost treasure, causing a storm, and even making oneself invisible or causing a tree to fall.

As discussed in chapter 2 of the preceding volume, every magickal ritual is composed of four time periods. The creation period of the evocation begins with the revelation that one must either obtain certain information, cause a storm, or what have you. This objective should be considered and meditated upon at length, and the appropriate demon must then be chosen to bring upon the desired results[1]. After making the carefully thought out decision regarding which demon to evoke, the preparation period begins. The original intention of the evocation should be recorded, and then forgotten about, until the time comes to compose the "interrogation of the spirit". The reason for this, is that all concentration should be focused on properly and efficiently completing the preparations, and on the performance itself, rather than being concerned with its outcome. The consideration of the expected results would direct energy away from the ritual itself, when all energies should be strictly devoted to the proper execution of the ritual, which requires one's full attention. There is no more effective manner of destroying one's chances for success in magickal ritual, then to consider the "lust of result".[2]

The requirements of the preparation period consists of the accomplishment of several tasks. The first and most important of which is the location of the temple. It should be located away from the general population, and the more secluded, the better. The circle may be constructed outside, theoretically, although the ideal setting would be within a closed dwelling. A house with neighbors closer that one half mile is not at all desirable, and an apartment building is completely out of the question. This restriction will undoubtedly dissuade the majority of practitioners who cannot afford such a luxury, however those of the art will realize that when there is will, there is always a way.

The magick circle must be constructed in an appropriate manner, not more than twenty four hours prior to the beginning of the "performance". It should be nine feet in width, and painted on the surface of the floor beforehand, as depicted in diagram #9[3]. The directions for the construction of the circle are described in Book two, chapter nine of the "Key of Solomon"[4] should first be followed, using the appropriate words and symbols, as illustrated in diagram #9. However, there is no need to assemble and exhort disciples, if none are available. Also, rather than sounding the trumpet, one may substitute the "Banishing ritual of the Serpent", as outlined in chapter 5 of the first volume. They should then follow the directions in Book one, chapter three of the "Key"[5]. The practitioner may once again skip the section regarding disciples, and before the prayers, one should perform both the "Lesser Banishing Ritual of the Pentagram" and the "Banishing Ritual of the Hexagram". Then continue with the prayers and conjurations that follow, which should be memorized; however, they may be written on properly prepared pages within a properly prepared notebook, and kept for reference. The prayers continue through the end of chapter four of Book one, where the magician may finish with a banishing ritual, release to the spirits, and lastly a closing. Afterwards, the magician will again enter the circle, and banish the area. They may then use properly prepared acrylic paint and brushes to paint the appropriate colors within the circle. The space between the circles where the serpent is drawn in should be bright yellow. The square in the center of the circle should be filled in with bright red. All outlines and lettering is black. The outer triangles of the hexagrams, where the letters A, D, O, N, A, and I are, should be filled in with yellow, and the center sections should be filled in blue around the crosses within. The outer triangles of the pentagrams outside of the diameter of the circle should be yellow, and the centers red.

The triangle outside the circle should be drawn in the direction corresponding to the elemental nature of the specific demon evoked[6]. It must be made at a two foot distance from the outer circumference of the circle. Also, each side must be three feet in length, and it must be somehow elevated three feet above the floor[7]. The base of the triangle is the side where the name "PRIMEUMATON" is written, and this side should always be positioned closest to the circle. The outline of the triangle and the name "MICHAEL" is in black, and the names outside the triangle written in red. The circle in the triangle should be filled in black, and the remaining spaces within the triangle should be white.

Another important requirement is that at least two people are necessary to perform a goetic evocation. Ideally both should be competent practitioners, who work well together as partners. It would be acceptable for as many as five people to participate, but no more than five. Additionally, there are stringent regulations concerning the apparel of all participating operators.

All individuals taking part must wear properly purified and consecrated clothing or "vestments". First, a robe of white natural cloth, such as cotton or silk. The design in diagram #10 must be embroidered in red silk thread at the breast of the robe. They must also wear white leather boots, with the design in diagram #11 drawn in red cinnabar[8]. Additionally, worn by all individuals participating is a three inch wide "girdle" or belt, traditionally of lion's skin, but any quality leather will suffice. The following four words should be inscribed in Hebrew on the "girdle": TETRAGRAMMATON, AHIH, ALIUN, ALUAH. Lastly, all must wear a leather hat with ALHIM inscribed in front, YHVH on back, ADNI on the right side, and AL on the left. As continually repeated, all materials used must, of course, be properly purified and consecrated.

Each person involved must also be armed with a magical dagger, inscribed with the symbols in diagram #12[9]. The handle of the dagger should be steel, and black in color. It should be between eight and fifteen inches in total length. Additionally, it should be purchased on a Saturday, and immediately properly purified and consecrated. Then one should say the following prayer over it:[10]

> "I conjure thee, YEHUWAU, by the authority of God, the Father almighty, by the virtue of Heaven and the stars, by the virtue of the angels, by that of the elements, by that of stones and herbs, and in like manner, by the virtue of snowstorms, thunder and winds, that thou receive all power unto the performance of those things, in the perfection of which we are concerned, the whole without trickery, falsehood or deception, by the command of God, Creator of the ages and emperor of the angels. Amen."

> "DAMAHI, LUMECH, GADEAL, PANCIA, VELOAS, MEOROD, LAMIDOCH, BALDOCH, ANERETHON, METATRON, most holy angels, be wardens of this instrument, because I shall make use of it for several necessary works."

It should then be purified and consecrated once again, before wrapping it in a black silk cloth. The cloth should have the symbols and names illustrated in diagram #13 embroidered on it, and as well purified and consecrated[11], as are all objects utilized in works of the art. The dagger should then be concealed in a secluded place for no less than thirty five days, and it must never be shown to anyone.

At least the primary operator must be additionally armed with a magickal sword, which should be over three feet long and inscribed[12] with the symbols in diagram #14. This sword should have been purchased on a Wednesday, and treated exactly as was the dagger. It would be advisable for all involved to possess both a dagger and sword, but this is not necessarily required.

Every individual should also possess the "Hexagram of Solomon", which is illustrated in diagram #15, and this must be drawn on properly purified and consecrated parchment paper, with properly prepared ink or paints. The outline is black, as are the words "TETRAGRAMMATON" and "TAU". The words "AGLA", "ALPHA" and "OMEGA" are in red letters. Five of the exterior triangles are filled in yellow, but the bottom-most triangle is left white, and the sigil is black. The center cross is red with the three little squares in black. This is to be worn at the waist level, presumably pinned or somehow affixed to the robe, and covered with white linen.

The primary operator must as well be in possession of the "Pentagram of Solomon". This is to be made on a three inch wide disk of either silver or gold, and etched or engraved with the sigil illustrated in diagram #16. Properly prepared ink should be used to color the names and sigils in black, and the word "TETRAGRAMMATON" in red. The center section should be painted green, and the outer triangles should be blue. The sigil of the specific demon, which is etched or engraved onto a disk made of the appropriate metal, is then affixed to the back side of this talisman[13]. These are to be worn about the neck of the primary operator by a thick silver chain, with a high quality safety catch.

Each individual should possess a shield or "magic ring", made of some metal; preferably silver or gold, although brass or copper would also suffice. This should be inscribed as in diagram #17, using properly prepared black paint.

The candles used for illumination during Goetic evocation should be made of beeswax, and only new candles should be used, having never been lit previously. They should be purchased on a Wednesday, and after purifying and consecrating, the following prayer should be recited over them:

"ENTABOR, NATABOR, SI TACIBOR, ADONAI, AN, LAYAMON, TINARMES, EOS, PHILODES. Angels of God, be present! I invoke you in my work, that I may obtain virtue by your mediation, and may be very surely perfected. I exorcise thee, creature of wax, and by the Creator and God almighty; who created all things from nothing, by His most holy name, and by His angels, I ordain thee to receive virtue and benediction in His name, so that thou may be sanctified and blessed, thus obtaining that virtue which we desire, by the most Holy name ADONAI, which is the life of all creatures."

The candle should then be engraved somehow[14] with the symbol in diagram #18. It should then be purified and consecrated once again, and wrapped in white silk cloth for at least seven days.

When these candles are first lit, the following prayer should be recited:

"I conjure thee, Oh creature of fire, in the name of the sovereign and eternal Lord, by His ineffable name, YOD, HEH VAU, HEH, by the name IAH, and by the name of power AL, that thou enlighten the heart of the spirits, which we shall call into the circle, so that they may appear before us without fraud and deceit, through the creator of all things."

Incense should be utilized in every operation. In the case of Goetic evocation, one would choose a suffumigation qabalistically appropriate to the nature of the specific demon chosen. Good quality Abramelin incense is suitable for the prelates or presidents, and solar demons or kings. Jasmine should be used for the marquises or lunar demons, benzoin would be best used for the dukes, tobacco would be suggested for the earls, and cedar for the princes.

The following prayer should be recited over the incense:

"Oh God of Abraham, Isaac and Jacob, vouchsafe to bless and sanctify these perfumes so that thy may obtain virtue and power to discern good spirits from bad, even phantoms and enemies, through thee, Oh ADONAI, who livest and reignest for ever and ever. Amen."

"Deign, Oh Lord, to sanctify this incense, so that it may become a signal remedy for the human race and the salvation of our souls and bodies, through the invocation of thy most Holy Name, YEHUWAU, so that all who inhale the smoke of this kind may have health of body and soul. Through the Lord who has created the ages of ages. So be it."

When lighting the incense, one would first recite the same prayer given for lighting the candles, and then continue with:

"ZAZAY, SALMAY, DALMAY, ANGERECTON, LEDRION, AMISOR, EUCHEY, OR! Great Angels, Angels of God be our help, and by you be our work fulfilled! And do thou also, ADONAI, be present and impart such virtue that this, (the designated spirit's name), may receive a form whereby our work may be accomplished."

All of these specific objects[15] and procedures contribute to the defense and safety of the operators. The symbols used are of a protective nature, and some are possibly the most potent sigils of protection ever devised. The student is advised to experiment with all of these symbols individually and in combination on the astral plane, recording all results, of course.

The appropriate day and time for the operation must be determined well in advance, according to certain criteria. Goetic evocations must be performed in the time frame between the new moon and full moon, and only when the moon is either 3, 5, 7, 9, 11 or 13 days old. It should be noted that the days given in the 1904 edition of the "Goetia" are purposely mistaken, presumably to insure that the practitioner is knowledgeable enough to recognize the misdirection.

The Marquises may only be bound on Monday, anytime from 3:00 PM to sunrise. Dukes must be bound on Friday, from sunrise to noon, and only in clear weather. Presidents must be bound on Wednesday, and only during sunlit hours. Earls may only be bound on Sunday or Monday, at any time of the day. Princes must be bound on Thursday, at any time of the day. The Knight may only be bound on Saturday, and only between dawn and sunrise, or between 4:00 PM to sunset.

The preparation will also include a purification period for the body of the magician himself. The exact date of the ritual should be determined at least forty-five days in advance. Thirty-five days prior to the operation, all individuals participating must begin the purification, in which they must abstain from all sexual activity. Additionally, they may partake of no red meat during this time, although fish and fowl is allowable over the first fifteen days. The practitioner should eat only vegetables, eggs and bread for the remaining twenty days, and drink only natural spring water.

Prior to this thirty five day purification, the magician should memorize the following prayer, which is to be recited every day of the period, once at noon, at 6:00 PM and midnight:

"Oh Lord God almighty, be thou favorable unto me, though unworthy to lift my eyes to Heaven, by reason of the multitude of my offences! Oh God all merciful, who wills not the death of a sinner, but rather his true conversion, bestow thy grace on me! Oh Lord our God, full of compassion, aide me in this work which I am about to perform, that thy name may be blessed forever! Amen."

Also during this period, one must bathe twice a day in hyssop treated natural water (spring or ocean). This should be upon waking in the morning, and before sleeping at night. During this ritual bathing, one should repeat the following prayer three times: "Asperges me, AHIEH (vibrate), Hyssoppo et mundabor. Lavabis me et super nivem dealbabor." The ritual bath is also to be performed prior to the construction of the circle, and also before the evocation itself.

The final construction of the circle should be completed less than twenty four hours prior to the beginning of the evocation. After this, the operators should all retire to private quarters, there to prepare the magickal weapons, meditate, perform numerous banishing rituals, and recite the purification prayer hourly, until bedtime. They should bathe once again before sleeping.

Thirty minutes before the ritual, every operator should begin the ritual bathing. After the bath, each operator promptly consecrates themselves by using their right forefinger to make the sign of the Rose Cross over their heart with Abramelin oil, while speaking these words of consecration: "Accendat in nobis ADNI (vibrate) ignem sui amoris et flammam aeternae caritatis."[16]

They should then don the robe, while saying:

"By the figurative mystery of this holy vestment, I will clothe me with the armour of salvation in the strength of the most high, ANCOR, AMACOR, AMIDEAS, THEODONIAS, ANITHOR, that my desired end may be effected through thy strength, Oh ADONAI! Unto whom the praise and glory will forever and ever belong. Amen."

They are now prepared to begin the operation.

DIAGRAM #9
Circle from figure #153 & #154 of the "Goetia"

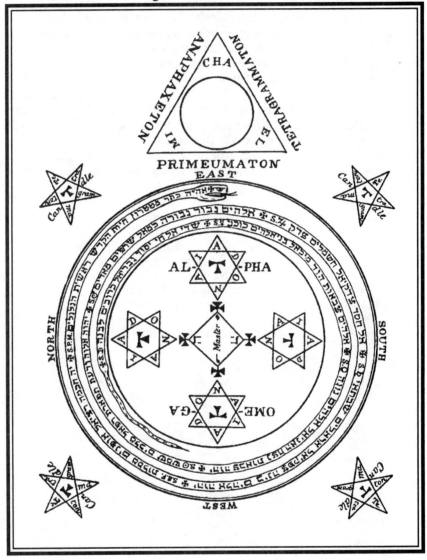

DIAGRAM #10
Design on robe

DIAGRAM #11
Design on boots

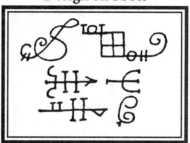

DIAGRAM #12
Symbols on dagger

DIAGRAM #13
Symbols on silk cloth

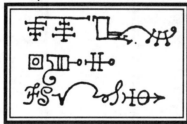

DIAGRAM #18
Symbol on candles

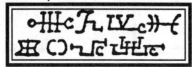

DIAGRAM #14
Symbols on sword

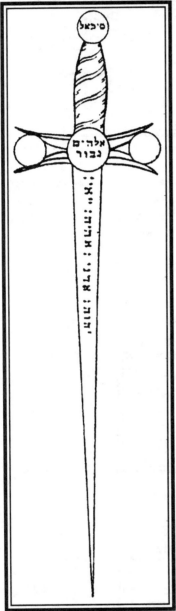

DIAGRAM #15
Hexagram of Solomon

DIAGRAM #16
Pentagram of Solomon

DIAGRAM #17
Disk or Magic RIng

DIAGRAM #19 - ALTAR SETUP

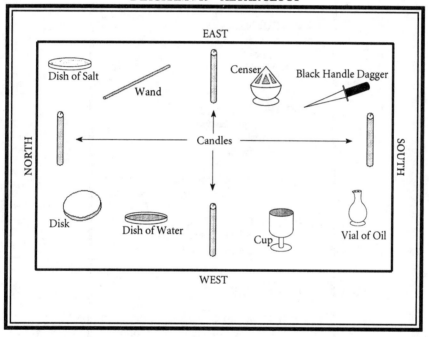

CHART # 28 - PREPARATIONS

PREPARATIONS

A. - TEMPLE
    1. location
    2. construction
        a. circle
        b. triangle

B. - VESTMENTS
    1. robe
    2. boots
    3. girdle
    4. hat

C. - WEAPONS
    1. dagger & sword
    2. disk
    3. symbols
        a. sigil
        b. Hexagram of Solomon
        c. Pentagram of Solomon

D. - ACCOUTERMENTS
    1. candles & candlesticks
    2. Incense & censer
    3. altar

E. - DAY & TIME

F. - PURIFICATION
    1. 35 days of abstinence & prayer
    2. construct an interrogation
    3. temple setup
    4. ritual bath
    5. donning vestments

7

THE PERFORMANCE

Section A

The detail of the preparation and performance may appear stringent, but the strict adherence to all of the given criteria is imperative. After all preliminaries dictated in the previous chapter have been completed, one is ready to proceed with the performance.

The primary operator enters the working area first, and immediately purifies and consecrates the circle. This is done by circumbulating deosil three times, within the inner circumference of the circle, while sprinkling properly prepared natural water, and speaking the words of purification. Then they should light the candles, and then the incense in the censer, speaking the appropriate words as described in the previous chapter. Then, while carrying the censer, they should circumbulate deosil three times, speaking the words of consecration.

The secondary operator and any others may then enter the circle area. The extraneous individuals will take their places standing in the center of any of the hexagrams, except the one closest to the triangle. Each should be dressed and armed as previously dictated, with magickal blade, disk and seal. They are not to move from their respective position for any reason.

The extraneous participants must all have duly followed the previously dictated prerequisites, being the purifications, bathings, consecrations and prayer. Novice practitioners or non-magicians should not be allowed to observe the proceeding, as their natural intolerance to the evocation could destroy any chances for success, as well as placing the lives of all participants in dire peril, should they attempt to leave or faint. Immediately prior to the operation, they should be made to swear the following oath:

> "I, (name and grade) do swear an oath that I have duly prepared for this operation exactly as instructed, and will observe silently and motionlessly from the spot where I am placed. I will not move, nor utter a single sound during the entire course of this operation, unless instructed to by either the primary or secondary operator. I am fully prepared to take all responsibility for my actions, and will never speak of any aspect of the events of this operation to any single person whatsoever. It is understood

121

that the consequences of breaking any part of this oath will inevitably result in my own destruction."

The primary and secondary operators stand together in the center square, where there should be an altar with the front facing the triangle.[1]

Immediately prior to the evocation, the primary operator should begin by striking the top of the altar eleven times with the butt of their dagger.[2] They should then state their name, grades (if any), and magickal motto.[3] Then they would state a pre-devised oath, stating the purpose of the evocation, and affirming that it will be completed.

Next the Lesser Banishing Ritual of the Pentagram, the Banishing Ritual of the Serpent[4], and the "Invocation of the Bornless One"[5] should be performed, in that order, by the primary operator.

The primary operator should then take their place, standing on the hexagram closest to the Triangle, staying within the confines of the protective circle. From the center of the circle, the secondary operator then recites the conjurations, obviously beginning with the first conjuration.[6] If the first recital of the first conjuration fails to produce immediate results, the operator should wait for approximately three minutes. If in that time, no presence is noted, it should be repeated, after which they should allow three more minutes to pass before a third recital, should nothing occur. If there are still no results after the third recital, proceed to the second conjuration in the same manner. If no presence is noted after three repetitions of the second, recite the third in the same manner, and then the "Invocation of the King", again, up to three times.

If at any point, the spirit's presence becomes noticeable, the secondary operator should first complete the conjuration in progress, and then begin "the address unto the spirit", reciting it in full, once. The spirit may not appear visibly at first, although its presence will become apparent immediately to the practitioner.[7]

If the third recital of the "Invocation to the King" produces no results, the "chain curse" or "spirit's chain" would ordinarily be performed. However, if the operator has never yet experienced a successful evocation, it is recommended that they discontinue the effort, and banish the area repeatedly. They should then record every aspect of the failed ritual, and begin to prepare for another attempt.

The operators should expect that the "chain curse" will be necessary, and prepare for such a circumstance.[8] The performance of this requires a few additional items be brought into the ritual. That being a source of fire, such as a small "Hibachi" grill, a pair of pliers, and a small metal box, painted black in fire-retardent acrylic. Also needed is an additional sigil of the spirit, on the appropriately corresponding metal. Lastly, a glass jar full of "things that bear a stinking smell", such as sulfur, camphor, or asafoetida. Every item must be duly purified and consecrated, as are all objects used in ritual. In addition, the following prayer should be read over this jar of "stinking things":

> "ADONAI, LAZAI, DALMAI, AIMA, ELOHI, by the invocation of thy most Holy Name, YEHUWAU, vouchsafe us the help of thy Grace, and may it assist us in all things which we need to fulfill; may all malice pass out herefrom, may it be blessed and sanctified in thy most powerful name. Amen."

Both of the operators should strive to prepare with even more diligence than they did for the previous experiment. Something was probably interfering with the proceeding, either the subconscious good sense of the practitioner, or possibly an outside force, not properly banished beforehand. It is also conceivable that the spirit was just unwilling, and strong enough to resist the forces of the evocation. In any case, one can never be too thorough in preparation.

They should then proceed with another attempt, using the three conjurations and the "Invocation of the King", exactly as earlier described. If no results are produced after this, they may perform the "chain curse or spirit's chain".

To begin the curse, the secondary operator first lights the fire, and then again recites the third conjuration. If still no presence is detected, they should add the first section of the curse, immediately following the conjuration. If still nothing occurs, they should then transfer the "stinking" contents of the jar into the black box, along with the spirit's sigil on a separate talisman. The box may then either be suspended over the fire, using wire held up with the sword, or just set on the metal grill, if using a simple "Hibachi". The operator would then recite the "conjuration of the fire" once. If still nothing occurs, they may continue with the "second curse", and then the "greater curse". If no results are produced during the reading of this curse, then the box should be placed immediately into the coals of the fire. If after two minutes, still nothing occurs, one may repeat the "greater curse" while the box lays in the coals.

If at any time the spirit does appear, or if its presence becomes noticeable, the curse should then be stopped, the box removed from the fire, and the talisman removed from the fire.[9] If after three repetitions of the "greater curse", still no results are produced, something is unquestionably amiss. The effort should be discontinued, and every aspect of the ritual must be examined, no matter how apparently trivial. It is the experience of the author that if these rituals are properly conducted, significant results do occur. These may not take place immediately; on the contrary, several attempts may be required. Persistence is the key. A magician will never progress if they are discouraged by failure. That is a part of the process. They must adapt to every situation, and have the ability to scrutinize a failed operation with objective reasoning to determine the cause of the failure, and then compensate. If it fails again, re-evaluate and re-compensate. It is a continuing process which must be endured though to the end, which will ideally result in one small success. That success is then evaluated, and more compensation is applied in the appropriate manner, and the successful result should improve. If not, re-evaluate and try again.[10]

The "address to the spirit" is to be recited by the secondary operator at the appropriate time, being the moment the spirit's presence is first apparent.[11] Following the address, the primary operator commands the spirit to appear "visibly and affably", and give true answers to the questions, which have been determined during the final stage of the preparation period. They should expect the spirit to be unwilling, impertinent and uncooperative. However, if it is properly imprisoned within the triangle, it will be at a great disadvantage.

If the spirit has not yet become visible, the secondary operator should repeat "the address", and then the primary operator should immediately follow by stating "I command thee to appear before me in a fair human shape, without any deformity or tortuosity, by the name IEHOVAH." The sword should be pointed towards the air above the triangle while making this statement, as if threatening the demon which should be present there. If the spirit still does not appear, at least partially, repeat the command using the names "IEHOVAH, TETRAGRAMMATON, ANAPHEXTON AND PRIMEUMATON." This should compel the spirit to either partial, or possibly full, appearance.[12]

If the spirit appears threatening, in some grotesque form, or screaming, repeat the command once again, using the four names given previously.

At visible appearance, the primary operator should recite the "welcome", after which he should extend the left hand, therein holding the pentacle, which is being worn around their neck, towards the spirit.[13] While pointing the pentacle at the spirit, the operator should then state forcibly, "BY THE

PENTACLE OF SOLOMON HAVE I CALLED THEE! GIVE UNTO ME A TRUE ANSWER.".

If the spirit appears docile and agreeable, or even if grudgingly restrained, you may proceed with the appropriate "initial interrogation". This should have been composed well in advance, during the preparation period. Every operation requires a unique interrogation, specifically constructed according to the purpose of the evocation, along with the known attributes of the individual entity.

The primary operator is expected to first interrogate the "prisoner", and then obtain its loyalty, however reluctantly. This is done by first verifying its identity as the proper spirit, or otherwise[14], and making the entity confess its true name and the numerical significance of its governing deity. One must also ascertain its current rank and title, governing astrological sign, and its office or designated magickal talents. Lastly, they must convince the spirit to divulge its "secret name", by which the operator may re-evoke the spirit with ease.

The demon will surely resist all efforts, but is likely to cooperate eventually, if sufficiently threatened with eternal torment and coerced by promises of release. Expect that it will attempt deception, and be prepared. The magician must be well educated in the hierarchy of both angelic, as well as demonic entities; for it will assuredly mislead them, if at all possible.

All dialogue between the primary operator and spirit should be duly recorded by the secondary operator, who should also stand prepared and able to take over, should it become necessary to do so. After the "initial interrogation" is completed, and the operator is certain of the identity of the spirit, one should then follow through with the interrogation regarding the purpose of the ritual. This should have also been conceived during the preparation period, at the same time as when the "initial interrogation" was devised.

With the purpose of the ritual accomplished, or information derived, the demon should lastly be instructed to swear an oath of allegiance to the primary operator. They should compel it to verbally declare the following:

"I, (name and title), do swear an oath, by the power of HOEHAI, to appear immediately upon being summoned by thee, through the name of (secret name), both visibly and affably, without deformity or tortuosity, to speak intelligibly to thine understanding, and make rational answers unto thine demands. I shall neither by deed nor action, allow or cause any harm to befall thee, nor any relation, companion, nor acquaintance thereof. I will remain bound by this oath for the remainder of my existence, and fully understand that the consequences of breaking this oath will result in mine eternal torment in fire unquenchable."

It has been suggested elsewhere in print that the primary operator should extend their sword through the protective circle, and compel the spirit to place its "hand" on the sword, while reciting the oath.[15] This act would prove a most fatal error. For no reason whatsoever should the sword, nor anything for that matter, be extended out of the circle during Goetic evocation. The circle's integrity would then be compromised, or to put it simply, the circle would be "broken". The resourceful demon may conceivably escape, possibly resulting in the destruction of the operator in the process, which would be a more desirable demise in comparison to the alternative possibility. An equally disastrous end would surely occur, should the demon contact the sword, while imprisoned within the triangle. Not only would the integrity of the triangle be compromised, in which case the spirit could escape with ease, the sword may act as a direct link to the operator, conveniently provided at that first moment of freedom.

The sword should remain in position between the spirit and the primary operator throughout the evocation, beginning from its first appearance, up to the moment of its disappearance from vision. Should the spirit somehow escape the triangle, and enter the circle, then the operators may attempt to defend themselves with dagger and sword; but never should the operator extend the sword beyond the boundaries of the protective circle.

After the oath is verbally recited by the demon, the operator commences with the "release" or "license to depart". After this recital, the spirit should disappear immediately. If it appears free from the triangle, but lingers, then recite the release again. If by the end of the second recital, the spirit has not departed, add, "By the names, YEHOWAU, ADONAI, EHIEH, ELOHIM, AGLA, ARARITA, I command thee to depart now!".

If it lingers still, the primary operator should perform the "Invocation of the Bornless One" within the confines of the circle. This invocation will surely result in the disappearance of the spirit.

After no traces of the spirit remains, the secondary operator should perform the "Lesser Banishing Ritual of the Pentagram", "Lesser Banishing Ritual of the Hexagram" and "Banishing Ritual of the Serpent", within the confines of the circle. The circle may then be broken, and all operators may withdraw to reflect on and discuss the evocation. They may use the time to transcribe records, or simply relax for a time. After no more than two hours, the circle area should be cleared of all evidence regarding the ritual. Then the area should be thoroughly cleaned, and repeatedly banished.

Every individual involved should then transcribe the most comprehensive records possible, regarding every aspect of the ritual, no matter how apparently trivial. Every remembered thought should be recorded before the end of that day. This should include a description of the events, the appearance and actions of the spirit, as well as the actions of the operators, the dialogue between operator and spirit, and also any memories and feelings of the individual should be recalled and noted.

Section B[16]

The First Conjuration[17]:

> I invoke and conjure thee (name), and fortified with the power of the Supreme Majesty, I strongly command thee by BARALAMENSIS, BALDACHEINSIS, PAUMACHIE, APOLORESEDES and the most potent princes GENIO, LIACHIDE, Ministers to the Tartarean Seat, chief princes of the seat of APOLOGIA in the ninth region; I exorcise and command thee, (name), by Him who spake and it was done, by the Most Holy and glorious Names ADONAI, EL, ELOHIM, ELOHE, ZEBAOTH, ELION, ESCHERCE, JAH, TETRAGRAMMATON, SDAI, do thou forthwith appear and show thyself to me, here before this circle, in a fair and human shape, without any deformity or horror; do thou come forthwith, from whatever part of the world, and make rational answers to my questions; come presently, come visibly, come affably, manifest that which I desire, being conjured by the Name of the Eternal, Living and True God, HELIOREM, I conjure thee also by the particular and true Name of thy God to whom thou owest thine obedience; by the name of the King who rules over thee, do thou come without tarrying; come, fulfill my desires; persist unto the end, according to mine intentions. I conjure thee by Him to whom all creatures are obedient, by this ineffable Name, TETRAGRAMMATON YEHOVA, by which the elements are overthrown, the air is shaken, the seas turned back, fire is generated, the earth moves and all the hosts of things celestial, of things terrestrial, of things infernal, do tremble and are confounded together; speak unto me visibly and affably in a clear, intelligible voice, free from ambiguity. Come therefore in the name ADONAI ZEBAOTH; come, why dost thou tarry? ADONAI SADAY, King of Kings commands thee.

The Second Conjuration:

I invoke, conjure and command thee, (name), to appear and show thyself visibly before this circle, in a fair and comely shape, without deformity or guile, by the Name of ON; by the Name YOD and VAU, which Adam heard and spake; by the Name JOTH, which Jacob learned from the angel on the night of his wrestling and was delivered of the hands of his brother Esau; by the Name of the God AGLA, which Lot heard and was saved with his family; by the Name ANEHEXETON, which Aaron spake and was made wise; by the Name SCHMES AMATHIA, which Joshua invoked and the Sun stayed it course; by the Name EMMANUEL which the three children Shadrak, Meshach and Abednego, chanted in the midst of the fiery furnace, and they were delivered; by the Name ALPHA and OMEGA, which Daniel uttered, and destroyed Bel and the Dragon; by the Name ZEBAOTH which Moses named, and all the rivers and waters in the land of Egypt brought forth frogs, which descended upon the houses of the Egyptians, destroying all things; by the Name ESCERCHIE ARISTON, which Moses named and all of the rivers and waters of the land of Egypt did turn into blood; by the Name ELION, which Moses called, and there fell a great hail; by the Name ADONAI, which Moses called, and locusts came and devoured what the hail had left; by the Name HAGIOS, by the seal of ADONAI, by those others, which are JETROS, ATHENOROS, PARACLETUS, by the three Holy and secret Names AGLA, ON, TETRAGRAMMATON; by the dreadful Day of Judgement; by the changing Sea of Glass which is before the Divine Majesty, mighty and powerful; by the four beasts before the Throne, by the fire which is about the Throne, by the Holy Angels of Heaven, by the Mighty Wisdom of God; by the seal of BASDATHEA, by this Name PRIMEMATUM, which Moses named, and the earth opened and swallowed Corah, Dathan and Abrim; do thou make faithful answers unto all my demands, and perform all my desires, so far as thine office shall permit. Come therefore peaceably and affably; come visibly and without delay; manifest that which I desire; speaking in a clear intelligible voice that I may understand thee.

The Third Conjuration:

I conjure thee, (name), by all the most glorious and efficacious Names of the Great and Incomprehensible Lord, the God of Hosts, come quickly and without delay, from whatsoever part of the world thou art in; make rational answers to my demands; come visibly, speak affably, speak intelligibly to my understanding. I conjure and constrain thee, (name), by all the aforesaid Names, as also by which Solomon bound thee and thy fellows in the brazen vessel, to wit, ADONAI, PRERAI, TETRAGRAMMATON, ANEXHEXETON, INESSENSATOAL, PATHUMATON, and ITEMON, do thou manifest thyself before this circle, fulfill my will in all things that may seem good to me. Be disobedient, refuse to come, and by the power of the Supreme Being, the Everlasting Lord, that God Who created thee and me, the whole world, with all contained therein, in 6 days; by EYE, by SARAY, by the virtue of the Name PRIMEMATUM, which commands the whole host of heavens; be disobedient, and behold I will curse thee and deprive thee of thine office, thy joy and thy place; I will bind thee in the depths of the bottomless pit, there to remain until the day of the Last Judgement. I will chain thee in the Lake of Eternal Fire and Brimstone, unless thou come quickly, appearing before this circle, to do my will. Come, therefore, in the Holy Names ADONAI, ZEBAOTH, AMIORAM; come, ADONAI commands thee.

The Invocation of the King:

O thou Great and Powerful King AMAYMON, who rules by the power of the Supreme God, EL, over all spirits, superior and inferior, but especially over the Infernal Order of the East, I invoke and command thee by the particular and true Name of God, by the God Whom thou dost worship, by the seal of thy creation, by the most mighty and powerful Name of God, JEHOVAH, TETRAGRAMMATON, Who cast thee out of heaven with the rest of the Infernal Spirits; by all the other potent and Great Names of God, creator of Heaven, Earth and Hell, of all contained therein; by their powers and virtues, by the Name PRIMEMATUM, which commands the whole Host of Heaven. Do thou force and compel (name) before this circle, in a fair and comely shape, without injury to myself or any creature, that he may give me true and faithful answer, so that I may accomplish my desired end, whatsoever it be, provided that it is proper to his office, by the power of the God EL, Who hath created and doth dispose of all things, celestial, aerial, terrestrial and infernal.

The Chain Curse or "Spirits Chain":

First Curse:
Thou wicked and disobedient (name), because thou hast not obeyed or regarded the words which I have rehearsed, the glorious and incomprehensible Names of the True God, Maker of all things, now I, by the power of these Names, which no creature can resist, do curse thee into the depths of the Bottomless Pit, to remain until the Day of Doom, in the Hell of unquenchable fire and brimstone, unless thou wilt forthwith appear in this triangle, before this circle, to do my will. Come, therefore, quickly and peaceably, by the Names ADONAI, ZEBAOTH, ADONAI, AMIORAM. Come, come, ADONAI, King of Kings, commands thee.

Conjuration of the Fire:
I conjure Thee, O Fire, by Him who made thee, and all other creatures in the world, to torment, burn and, consume this spirit (name) everlastingly.

Second Curse:
Because thou art disobedient, and obeyed not my commandments nor the precepts of the Lord thy God, now I, who am the servant of the Most High and Imperial Lord God of hosts, JEHOVAH, having this celestial power and permission, for this thine averseness and contempt, thy great disobedience and rebellion, will excommunicate thee, will destroy thy name and seal, which I have in this box, will burn them with unquenchable fire and bury them in unending oblivion, unless thou comest immediately, visibly and affably, here before this circle, within this triangle, assuming a fair and comely form, doing no harm unto me or any creature whatsoever, but giving reasonable answers to my requests and performing my desire in all things.

Greater Curse:
Thou art still pernicious and disobedient, willing not to appear and inform me upon that which I desire to know; now therefore, in the Name and by the power and by the dignity of the Omnipotent and immortal Lord God of Hosts, JEHOVAH, TETRAGRAMMATON, sole creator of Heaven, Earth and Hell, with all that is contained therein, the Disposer of all things, visible and invisible, I do hereby curse and deprive thee of all thine office, power and place; I bind thee in the depth of the Bottomless Pit, there to remain to unto the Day of Judgement, in the Lake of Fire and Brimstone, prepared for rebellious Spirits. May all the company of Heaven curse thee; may the Sun, the Moon, the Stars, the Light of the Hosts of Heaven, curse thee into fire unquenchable; into torments unspeakable; and even as thy name and seal are bound up in this box, to be choked with sulphureous and stinking substances, and to burn in this material fire, so, in the Name of JEHOVAH, and by the power and dignity of the three Names, TETRAGRAMMATON, ANEHEXETON, PRIMEMATUM, may all these drive thee, (name), into the Lake of Fire, prepared for the damned and accursed spirits, there to remain until the Day of Doom, remembered no more before the Face of that God, Who shall come to judge the quick and the dead, with the whole world, by fire.

The Address unto the Spirit:

Behold thy confusion if thou be disobedient. Behold the Pentacles of Solomon, which I have brought into thy presence. Behold the person of the Exorcist, who is called OCTINIMOS, in the middle of Exorcism, armed by God and fearless, potently invoking and calling. Make, therefore, reasonable answers to my demands; be obedient unto me, thy master, in the Name of the Lord BATHAL, rushing upon ABRAC, ABEOR, coming upon BEROR.

The Welcome:

Welcome, (name), welcome thou art unto me; I have called thee through Him who created Heaven, Earth and Hell, with all contained therein, and thou hast obeyed; also by the like power, I bind thee to remain affably and visibly before this circle, within this triangle, so long as I need thee, to depart not without my licence, until thou hast truly and faithfully fulfilled all that I shall require.

BY THE PENTACLE OF SOLOMON HAVE I CALLED THEE! GIVE UNTO ME A TRUE ANSWER.

The License to Depart:

(Spirit's name), because thou hast diligently answered My demands; I do hereby license thee to depart, without injury to man or beast; Depart, I say, and be thou willing and ready to come, whensoever duly exorcised and conjured by the Sacred Rites of Magic. I conjure thee to withdraw peaceably and quietly, and may the peace of God continue forever between thee and me. AMEN.

8

GOETIC EXPERIMENTS #1 - #5

The author's associate and partner has requested to remain anonymous, and will only be referred to by the initials S.H. Both operators kept separate records of the experiments, and the data quoted in this book are from the author's records only. All of the lengthy quotes and dialogue transcribed here were originally documented over five years previously, in penned longhand, which in places was barely legible, with little punctuation, and no paragraphs defined. These have been edited, and in places expounded upon, at the time of transcription.

Preparations for the series of Goetic experiments began in January of 1985, and the first experiment was conducted in early May of that same year. The demon #26, Bim, was chosen for evocation, and his sigil was etched on a copper disk, after the appropriate preparations were conducted with all materials used.

From the instructions outlined in chapter 6, we realize that dukes may only be evoked from sunrise to noon, and in clear weather. The day must be before the full moon, on an odd numbered day from the new moon. The dukes are ruled by Venus, so the day must be a Friday. It was also determined that Abramelin incense would be appropriate to use during the ritual; as Bim is a day demon, under the rule of the sign Sagittarius. Lignum aloe would be suggested for Sagittarian operations, and properly prepared Abramelin incense is lignum aloe based.

Every goetic evocation recorded was performed in a closed room, approximately 35 feet in length, 25 feet in width, and 10 feet in height. The walls were of modern drywall and plaster, soundproofed with double sheets of styrofoam and doubled drywall sheets. The circle was constructed on two sections of 12 foot by 6 foot by 1/2 inch plywood, which was hinged together to form a 12 foot square.[1] The corners were through bolted with 6 inch by 3/4 inch stainless steel hex head concrete screws, and anchored into the foundation of the dwelling. The circle was first drawn and consecrated, as was detailed in chapter six. The triangle was drawn on a separate 5 foot square piece of 1/2 inch plywood, and elevated 3 feet above the ground, anchored to the top of a wooden square, constructed from sections of 3/4 inch plywood and aluminum angle brackets, with dimensions of 5' x 5' x 3'. This square was anchored to a 6 foot square piece of 1/2 inch plywood,

133

which was throughbolted and anchored into the foundation. The triangle was placed in the east, two feet from the outer diameter of the circle, as is appropriate for the evocation of a duke. All material used were of course, properly purified and consecrated before-hand.

The dwelling was unfortunately located in a relatively populated community, which proved, as should be expected, detrimental to any long term neighbourly relations.

At first, the author found it highly inconvenient to completely memorize the lengthy conjurations, curses and restraints of the "Goetia". All were transcribed onto a quality bond paper, duly purified and consecrated, and placed in a prepared three ring binder, for use in the circle. Unfortunately, few significant results were recorded during any evocation in which the dialogue was read from pages. In fact, the first four experiments conducted were virtually uneventful.

The fifth attempt to evoke Bim produced the authors first, albeit brief, contact with an entity whose mere suggestion of presence, even for the two to three seconds in which the event occurred, would affect most individuals quite tragically. As prepared as he was, the event resulted in an apprehension which delayed the sixth experiment for just over eight months. The following is an excerpt from the records of November 15, 1985, during the fifth attempted evocation of the demon, Bim:

> During the second reading of the second conjuration, while speaking the sentence "...by the fire round about the throne; by the holy angels of Heaven; and by the mighty wisdom of God; I do potently exorcise thee that thou appearest here before the circle..."; from the direction of the east, came a sound in the volume of a deafening thunder clap directly overhead. It was the two words "You fools!", in what could not be described as a "voice" in any sense of the word. It was an extremely guttural baritone, with a resonance that struck both S.H. and myself to the very core of our being.

> Although no visible appearance took form, we were both stricken with a nameless fear. The primal instinct of a man when encountering a being of demonic nature stimulates terror and loathing, which must be overcome eventually, but neither S.H. nor I have ever experienced such a presence, a power or force not of the world which man usually dwells.[2] Perhaps a form of concentrated evil, although words fail to capture this feeling of dread and disgust. One could never prepare themselves effectively to initially encounter this experience with no desire to flee and hide from such a horrible fate, at the clutches of a demon spawn from hell.

We immediately ceased the evocation, then shakily performed the release and closing, and proceeded to banish the circle area with the Lesser Banishing Ritual of the Pentagram, the Lesser Banishing Ritual of the Hexagram, the Banishing Ritual of the serpent, and The Star Ruby. But afterwards, a dark presence hung in the air of our temple, like a dense cloud or fog. Hated, diseased, unseen, the feeling of a soul tortured and tormented over countless eons of eternal and infernal damnation.

An hour later, after S.H. had departed wearily, I returned and banished the area with the same four banishing rituals, and then using each planetary banishing hexagram. After another hour, I returned once again, and due to fatigue, performed just the Banishing Ritual of the Serpent and the Star Ruby. (end entry)

The dark presence loomed in the temple for approximately twelve days, surviving well over one hundred well performed banishing rituals, before becoming unnoticeable. This may be described as an astral "fog", which seemed to permeate the area, apparently seeping into other areas of the dwelling. Several visitors commented on experiencing an "uneasy feeling" in other rooms, and some mild poltergeist activity did occur during the twelve day period. No severe reactions were recorded, however, and after this period, things seemed to return to "normal".

9

GOETIC EXPERIMENTS #6 - #8

For the sixth experiment, which was conducted on Friday, July 18th, 1986, S.H. and the author again attempted to evoke Bim, who has been the subject of all five previous experiments. This attempt was eventless, as was the seventh.[1]

The eighth was the first in which we incorporated "the black box"[2] described in "the General Curse, called the spirits' chain" of "The Goetia", and this experiment was the second to record audible results. Also incorporated into the circle was a small Hibachi, a glass jar full of a mixture of sulphur powder and camphor leaves, and a pair of pliers. Both it and the black box were acquired on a Tuesday, and properly purified, consecrated and wrapped in black cloth, to be concealed for 35 days in a secluded place, before their first use.

The second audible reaction occurred during the first reading of the "conjuration of the fire", approximately thirty seconds after inserting Bim's sigil etched on a copper disk into the black box, which was lined with the sulfur and camphor mixture, and then setting the box on the grill above the coals burning in the Hibachi. The following is an excerpt taken from the records dated December 12, 1986:

> During the first reading of the "conjuration of the fire", while speaking the sentence "...and shall burn thee in the immortal fire and bury thee in immortal oblivion;...", another thunderclap occurred, although not quite so deafening as that experienced during experiment #5, and seemingly emanating from the triangle in the east. The same guttural baritone vibrated "Learn the Words!". This time, we were prepared, although somewhat slightly fatigued from a combination of breathing the noxious fumes emanating from the black box over the hot coals, and repressing that ever present primal urge to retreat from a supernatural presence of being.
>
> We repeated the curse and left the sigil in the black box, until the third attempt produced no effects whatsoever. We then performed the release and closing, and the Lesser Banishing Ritual of the Pentagram, the Lesser Banishing Ritual of the Hexagram, the Banishing Ritual of the Serpent and the Star Ruby.

Without exiting the circle area, I removed the black box from the coals, removed the copper disk with pliers, and emptied the contents on to the coals, which sparked an extremely noxious smoke. We then left the circle area and allowed the materials to burn completely within the confines of the circle, until the ashes mixed with those of the coals. We then returned and thoroughly aired out the room with electric fans. We then burned copious amounts of Abramelin incense, and afterwards we burned copious amounts of a musk and myrrh mixture.

Several hours later, I returned and banished the area with the same four banishing rituals previously performed. I then collected every bit of the ashes from the Hibachi, transported them to the nearby ocean, and allowed them to blow away, mixing with the beach sand and sea water. I then returned to the circle area, and banished four times once again, and then used each planetary banishing hexagram. (end entry)

Afterwards, a familiar presence lingered in the area. This time, it was predominantly noticeable for six days, surviving over fifty banishing rituals, and could only be barely sensed for about two days following that. The sensation was virtually identical to the residual effects left from the fifth experiment, although no poltergeist activity was noted, and no visitors remarked on any unusual feelings. From the lessened length of time that the presence was observed, it was assumed that either the effect was not quite as strong as previously experienced, or the thorough banishings proved somewhat more effective than before.

10

GOETIC EXPERIMENT #9

After an hour long discussion a few days after experiment #8, S.H. and the author both decided that they should memorize each of the lengthy conjurations, curses, and restraints[1] before proceeding with the ninth experiment. They had still not successfully evoked the demon Bim to visual appearance, and since the ritual magician must always finish that which he begins, it was not a matter of choice over which to debate.

Due to the fairly substantial amount of time required to memorize the nine pages of ritual, and the various projects they both were working on, nearly five months passed before the ninth experiment actually took place. But on May 8, 1987, they dared once again to enter the circle area, more prepared then they had ever been. Armed with their swords and magic rings[2], "the black box", and two sigils of Bim, properly etched on properly prepared copper disks. One had the silver pentagram of Solomon attached to the back, and was worn about the author's neck by a thick silver rope chain. The other disk was prepared in advance, in case the necessity arose to use "the black box", which was also included, along with the "Hibachi", jar of sulphur and camphor mix, and pliers.

The preliminary ritual were duly performed, as they were in all previous experiments. The author performed the purifications, consecrations and banishings, and then the secondary operator entered the circle, and took his place in the center of the circle.

The following is from the records:

S.H. commenced with the first conjuration, and repeated it thrice, with no results. I stood on the hexagram to the east side of the circle, near the triangle with my sword drawn. The proper interrogation fixed in my mind, and also each conjuration and curse memorized, in case the necessity arose for me to take over. S.H. continued with the second conjuration, and repeated it thrice, with no results. He continued through three repetitions of both the third, and then the "Invocation of the King".

He then began the "chain curse" by lighting the fire of the "Hibachi", which had been prepared with standard self-lighting charcoal. He recited the third conjuration once again, followed by the first curse, with no results. Then, he placed the camphor and sulfur combination into the box, and the extra copper sigil of "Bim". The box was then set on the grill of the "Hibachi".

He continued with the "conjuration of the fire", the "second curse", and then began the recital of the "greater curse". After finishing the first sentence "Thou art still pernicious and disobedient, willing not to appear and inform me upon that which I desire to know;...", a thick gray mist began to rise from the very center of the black circle in the triangle, as if emanating from a small hole in the center. S.H. noticed the mist, but determinedly continued reciting the curse all the way through. He stopped without repeating, and I assume he was staring intently as I was, though he was behind me. I noted that he did cease the recital, but not knowing at all what to expect in the next minutes, I prepared myself as best I could.

S.H. then quickly removed the sigil from the "black box", using the pliers, and removed the box from the grill. Transfixed, my eyes locked on the phenomenon which we had begun to prepare for some twenty seven months prior. The thick mist or vapor rose slowly, much slower than smoke would naturally rise. By the time S.H. had finished the reading of the "greater curse", it had risen to a height of approximately two feet. It fanned out as it rose, in a funnel shape, still very fine at the floor level, spreading outward in a lazy curving inward arc, to a width of about twelve to thirteen inches near the top.

Two to three minutes after S.H. finished speaking, the mist had risen to a height of about four feet. The base was still a very narrow stream, although appearing as dense smoke which thinned out as it spread upwards and outwards. As this was occurring, the black circle in the triangle appeared to become liquid or gel-like, starting from the center of the circle, where the smoke or vapor seemed to be emitted from a small "hole" about an inch in diameter. The gel-effect spread outward, until the whole black circle took on the appearance of a thick, black pool of ink. I also noticed a slight convex effect, as if some pressure from beneath the triangle was pushing upward. By this time, approximately six minutes had passed since S.H. stopped speaking, the mist had risen to a height of about five feet, spreading out some twenty five inches in width. The base still appeared to be about one inch thick, but very dense in consistency.

We spoke in hushed tones, me over my shoulder without taking my eyes from the phenomenon, or lowering my sword from pointing directly at its center. S.H. asked me if I could handle it, or should he move forward by my side. I told him to stand ready, but hold fast. My brass shield or "magic ring" was on the ground at my feet, and I reached down with my left hand for it, keeping the sword in my right. I stood prepared, or so I thought. But this was my first direct encounter with a force not of the world as we know it, but of another world. A dark, violent wasteland, which is not even conceivable but to a very, very few humans who dare to open gates no man should tamper with. The forces unleashed might at any moment overcome the operator, should some unforeseen difficulty arise at a crucial moment. Was I prepared? Well, I survived to write these records, so it must be safe to assume that I was, at least, partially prepared. Although, I assuredly knew not what to expect.

The apparition had risen to a height of just over six feet from the top of the triangle[3], which caused it to near the ceiling of the room. It had spread to a width of approximately thirty five inches near the top. There was still very little definition of solidity, and the shape was definitely that of a funnel-cloud, its edges arching rather than being straight.

S.H. began reciting the "address unto the spirit, etc.", and after speaking the sentence "BATHAL or VASHAT rushing upon ABRAC! ABEOR coming upon ABERER!", the mist seemed to begin a rotation to the right or counterclockwise, first slowly, but then faster. I hesitated and observed as the rotation increased in velocity. I could not calculate the speed of rotation, as the lower portion seemed to rotate faster than the top, in a whirlwind effect, but an estimation would be one to two revolutions per second, at it's fastest. The motion did draw in air from behind and around me, causing noticeable and unusual currents. Also, the temperature of the room dropped noticably, possibly by about 10 - 15 degrees.

By the time three minutes had passed, after completing the "address", the air movement in the room was becoming quite a distraction. My hair is well past shoulder-length, and swirling around my head, threatening my sidereal vision, as well as occasionally hindering frontal vision. This is a definite disadvantage, noted for future reference to either cut hair or tie back.

The grey mist was now swirling rapidly in a definite funnel shape, and a form began to appear within the greyness. It first appeared approximately four minutes after S.H. finished the recital of the "address", as a small point of color in the greyness. The color was not discernable at first, but soon became noticeable as a small dot of grayish purple or mauve. Some effect was taking shape within the swirling cloud, starting as a shapeless spot of color, but then seeming to stretch upward and downward into a thickening line of faint coloring. Spreading further in all directions, the color deepened, although the form was not discernable as any specific shape for a period of twenty to thirty seconds.

The grey mist was partially concealing some entity within its swirlings. I took notice that the black circle within the triangle was still exhibiting a convex effect, and the surface of the circle had taken on the appearance of a black semiliquid or gel, seemingly pulsing or oozing from some pressure beneath its surface. The base of the funnel cloud had now spread out over a space of six to eight inches, and the mist was allowing a bit more visibility as the speed of the rotation increased. I then noticed a definite form within the swirlings, and the color of mauve deepened behind the grey mist.

Then, in a sudden flash, the mauve coloring exploded outward before me, temporarily flooding my vision so I could perceive only that color for several seconds, as if a blanket had suddenly been thrown over my head. As my sight returned fairly quickly, the room and everything in my vision was bathed in a mauve light.[4]

Looking before me, the room was bathed in a seemingly glowing light, and the grey mists was still swirling rapidly before me in the funnel-cloud formation. At six inches above my own eye level[5], there appeared a face peering through the mist. I could clearly discern the features of a wolf-like face, with a sickly blue coloring, and two short horns between pointed ears. The eyes were a bright yellow, with no sign of pupils, glaring down at me in disgust.

I pointed my sword directly at the face, and stated firmly "I command thee to appear before me in a fair human shape, without any deformity or tortuosity, by the name IEHOVAH." By the time I spoke the words "fair human shape", a small whine began to emit from the face, which grew into an ear piercing roar, that resounded within the walls of the room, something like that of a lion in great pain. After which, the face withdrew back into the mist.[6]

I repeated the command, using the names IEHOVAH, TETRAGRAMMATON, ANAPHEXTON and PRIMEUMATON. Although the face did not reappear, a somewhat subdued, but still quite loud, baritone voice painfully spoke, "Why does thou torture me so?". While still pointing the sword with my right hand, and holding the disk in my left, I replied, "I command thee to appear before me now, visibly and affably, or your torment will be eternal.". A muscular blue arm and clawed hand reached outward from the mist, swiping at the air, then quickly withdrew. At the same moment, the baritone boomed out, "You are not my master!".

I then inhaled very deeply, and began a series of names, all vibrated to the highest pitch that I could possibly reach. These were : YHVH, ADNI, ALHIM, AGLA, TZABAOTH SHADDAI, ELIM, AL, YAH, TETRAGRAMMATON, ANAPHEXTON, PRIMEUMATON, YESHIMON, HESION, ANABONA, YOD and VAU. I'm not sure exactly why I used these names in this order, but it somehow came to me at the moment.[7] I continued to point the sword at the spot where the face had been, and held the disk in my left hand.

There was then the sounds of loud growling, turning into a moan, emitting from the vapors. Then the following words were spoken: "I will speak with thee.". I replied "Then show thyself, and state your name and office.". "I do not choose to show myself, nor reveal my name. I said that I would speak with thee." was the response, from a deep voice that appeared to originate from the east, but resounded in my head, with a mild echo effect. I said, "I command thee to show thyself, and reveal to me your name and office.". The obstinate reply came, "No!".

Feeling even a bit arrogant to have finally succeeded in my endeavor, I commanded once again, "I command thee to show thyself, by the power of (same fourteen names in same order).".

By the time I vibrated the word "VAU", a low whine began and grew into another lion's roar, which terminated suddenly as a face did appear at the edges of the mist above the triangle. It glared down at me again, as it had a few moments ago, with a foul and contemptuous expression, scowling through pupil-less yellow eyes. The bluish skin coloring was sickly and patchy, resembling somewhat the flesh of a corpse, with some animated quality, which I can not find words to describe.

My sword had been pointing at that same place since its first appearance, in my right hand. My intention was to utilize my most effective poker-face, however I am not sure if I succeeded. I recited the "welcome", and then moved close to the edge of the circle and said "By the pentacle of Solomon have I called thee! Give unto me a true answer.". As I spoke, I used the disk in my left hand to hold the talisman on the chain around my neck extended forward. This was so I would not have to lower the disk, and also kept it up high before me, in case it was needed to protect my face.

"And who might you be?" was the response from the voice out of the east. I assume that it was this spirit, although the mouth did not open to speak. The words resounded still in my head, and the eyes seemed to regard me and the surroundings. "I ask the questions now. What is your name and office?" was my reply, becoming somewhat aggravated with the obstinence. I would say that in this case, that reaction is preferable to being scared witless, which would be the sane person's normal response. "I am known by many names." came the voice into my head.[8]

My retort was, "I grow tired of your disobedience and belligerence. Tell me now your name, or the torment begins." I drew another deep breath, and again vibrated those same fourteen names in the highest pitch I could manage.

The eyes winced slightly, and the voice proclaimed "I have been called Turel by some, and ..."

I interrupted by calling out, "False! You are surely not Turael, messenger of Jupiter. Your lies will not be tolerated, and if you do not give unto me a true answer,..."

143

The voice interrupted, "Bomashijael is my true name. What is it that thou would have of me?"

I answered, "Firstly, give unto me thy true name. Your attempted deception will result in the greatest imaginable suffering by unquenchable..."

The voice again interrupted, "I have given you my name. It is truly Bomashjael, and I am ruled over by the sign of the archer. Now set me free!"

"You are in no position to make demands. If Bomashijael is your true name, and being of Sagittarian nature, what number controls thee?" was my response.

"Do you not already know? You who proposes to be one capable of controlling me. I could destroy you in an instant..."

I interrupted again "My power seems to hold you imprisoned now, does it not? Destroy me then, if you are able.". I was answered by more growling, and the eyes narrowed as if staring intently, but I was not affected. "You seem to be sparing me, for some odd reason. Shall we make friends?", I continued.

"What does thou mean by those words? You speak in riddles, and I cannot answer truly to such rhetoric." was his subdued response.

"Then tell me: what number controls thee?", I commanded forcibly. "Nineteen." was the curt response. I replied, "So you are Bomashijael, the Sagittary, and controlled by the power of nineteen, and by he who is represented by that number. Of this you are certain, for if you falsely claim...". "That be my true name and nature." he interrupted. "Then by what name shall I control you?" I inquired. "Never shall I reveal that to you!" he proclaimed. "You are both obstinate and pernicious. Must I torment you for all eternity? If need be, that is exactly what I shall do." I raged. My boldness surprised me afterwards, and I felt as my actions throughout the experience were not necessarily my own. I was somehow guided, and that who was performing the experiment was some alter-personality. I apparently began speaking in a more archaic manner, and in reflection, experienced more anger than I would normally. My attitude became that of a stronger and more potent practitioner than I admittedly was. This may be some instinctive response to the danger, as weakness or hesitation in such an affair may be highly detrimental, and I felt absolutely no fear during this episode. In fact, I was strangely elated and stimulated. The stimulation was not so much adrenal, as egotistic. Now later, I felt that I had not been "myself" at the time, at least not during the most intense interrogation.

I called over my shoulder for S.H. to prepare the "black box" once again, but he was halted by the demon before retrieving the box.[9]

I then stated, "Then you are Bomashijael, the Sagittary, who is controlled by the power of he who is represented by the number nineteen, and I may control thee by the name ------."

"Those words are true." came the reply.

Throughout the course of this dialogue, the whole room remained bathed in the faint mauve glow, which first manifested at the initial appearance of the face over the triangle. Since that time, I had been standing before the triangle, holding the sword in my right hand pointed at the face, and the disk in my left hand, ready to raise before my face, if necessary.

"Then what is your title and office?", I inquired.

The spirit replied, "Since you do possess the abilities to perform that which you now do, surely you must know of my status, and peculiar talents."

"I desire to know more, much more.", was my response.

Spirit: "And what is it that you desire?" Operator: "I have already said that it is I who will ask the questions." Spirit: "Then ask!" Operator: "What is your title and office?" Spirit: "I preside over thirty nine legions of Arab-Zaraq, as sovereign arch-duke in the dominion of Amaimon." Operator: "And your office?" Spirit: "My office lies mainly in dealings with the dead. I am able to animate corpses, and compel them to discuss their former lives. I can also gather them together, to create armies of rotting flesh. Also, I teach the art of necromancy." Operator: "Is this all that you are capable of?" Spirit: "I have several secondary offices as well." Operator: "What are they?" Spirit: "I may answer truly any question regarding all the mysteries of nature. I can bestow the gift of eloquence, and the ability to speak eloquently. I am also capable of causing women to fall in love, as well as men." Operator: "It has been said that you also bestow riches and wealth on those able to bind thee." Spirit: "This was true once, but over time, the desire for material wealth became an obsolete value, as power is the true measure of superiority. Even the mightiest of mortal men have possessed no wealth; such was the case of the Nazarite, Christ, who has been worshipped as a God by your kind for two thousand years after his passing. Because men were plainly capable of obtaining wealth without assistance, and we have no use for modern currency, the matter evolved into one concerned with only by man. Others of us are adept at locating lost treasures, however one may have to travel over great distances, as few treasures remain lost indefinitely. Those few may be difficult to obtain, even after being located."

145

I was slightly taken back by this in-depth response. Previously, all answers had been matter-of-fact, short, curt, one sentence statements, not disclosing anything other than that requested. I quickly asserted that this rhetoric was meant to be misleading, although I did not persist in this line of questioning. What I came to assume was that with the introduction of printed currency, spirits lost the ability to establish wealth through illusion or deception. This may have been due to the comprehensive documentation of financial matters, as well as the strict regulation of the quantity of currency printed. Of course, the ego of the spirit would never allow it to admit having lost the ability to control matters of wealth, but instead managed to side-stepped the issue in true political form.[10] To acquire financial assistance was a secondary factor in the choosing of this spirit, however I proceeded undaunted with the previously established inter-rogation, which focused on the primary intention to obtain certain information.

Operator: "It has been said that you have considerable understanding of the nature and virtues of spirits and dead souls, and also of the worlds in which they dwell."

Spirit: "The art of necromancy is complex indeed; although surely one capable of raising my spirit must possess the required talents to learn. If you would release me, I will demonstrate..."

Operator: "You are now properly bound, and will remain so until I am satisfied with your answers. Your ridiculous attempts at deception and trickery are a great annoyance, and the consequences will surely cause you to regret this insolence. I have specific questions to which I demand that you answer truly."

What followed was approximately ten more pages of verbal banter, as well as numerous veiled (and some not so veiled) and personal insults, along with a good deal of distasteful rhetoric. Very little useful data was extracted from these pages of writings, so at this point, we will end the chapter, and the author will attempt to clarify certain aspects of the spirit's general philosophies in chapter 12. It should be noted that the demon often attempts to convince the operator to "release him". However, it is of the utmost importance that the operator never releases the spirit before the conclusion of the planned interrogation, and after having them verbally proclaim the oath, as dictated in chapter 7.

11

THE RESULTS

The complete records of the series of Goetic experiments conducted by the author and his associate, occupies two 8" x 10" three ringed binders, totalling well over five hundred pages. However, the large majority of these records must never be printed, as a substantial amount of the data deals with instructions for black magick ritual. If any of this material should aid another in the practice of the black arts, the karmic repercussions would inevitably return to the author. Also recorded were various statements of highly personal nature to the author, as well as his partner. Some of the data recorded could prove extremely detrimental to the lives of numerous individuals, not to mention that of the author. Additionally, much of what was discussed with these spirits, in general, must be taken with a large grain of salt. Of the twenty four experiments, seven were completely eventless, three resulted in vocal contact only, six resulted in partial materializations, and on eight occasions, the designated spirits manifested in full form apparition. None of these spirits appeared in the forms described in "The Goetia". They all appeared in various humanoid shapes, ranging from skeletal to obese. Each apparition had eyes glowing bright yellow, with no visible pupils present. Each had bluish, somewhat decayed-appearing skin, prominent pointed teeth and fangs, clawed hands, protruding foreheads, and all had two short horns above the forehead. They also had snouts, rather than noses, as well as pointed ears set high on their heads, and unusually pointed chins. Several specific facial features did vary considerably with the individual spirits, such as the face's shape, skin tone and distinquishing marks. Also, each seemed capable of altering the shape and form of their presented appearance.

Their voices ranged vastly, from deep baritones to high pitched sopranos. Each word echoed and vibrated, seemingly "inside" the operators head. In fact, the author is presently unaware if the voices were audible to the world outside of the working area. Although the immediate neighbors did make mention of unusual noises emanating from the dwelling during our experiments[1], they did not specify that these sounds resembled spoken voices. Fortunately, the author's rock band frequently rehearsed near the working area, and the neighbors were apparently satisfied by the explanation that the noises came from a "Moog" synthesizer

Certain events remained consistent throughout each experiment. These include the strange mauve luminosity that permeated the working area, which was explained as the escape of some of the atmosphere from the demonic world, through the "gate", which the demon was drawn through. This mixed with the light of our working area to produce the mauve effect. The funnel shaped cloud over the triangle was also present during each experiment, as was the convex effect of the black circle, and the presence of an oozing, semi-liquid substance. The presence of the strange air currents, as well as unusual electrical power surges were also consistent during each experiment, and also the noticable drop in room temperature.

We had succeeded in evoking Bim, Gimaliel, Andrealphus, Halphus, Shax, Gamigin, Naberius and Malphus. The twenty-fourth and final experiment, in which we attempted to evoke Furcas, resulted in somewhat disastrous effects, terminating in what could only be described as a small explosion in our working area. This convinced the author of his inadequacy of proper location. A somewhat milder revelation was the fact that he neglected his living necessities in order to make time to study and practice. He became aware that his financial stability was crucial to any further experimentation, and has discontinued Goetic experiments until such time when he can procure a suitable location to practice.

Although the expected results of the author's first evocation was primarily to obtain certain information, and secondly to obtain wealth, as it turns out, no treasure is obtainable through the goetic demons. They have no power over modern financial institutions, nor do they have the ability to produce jewels or cause ancient gold coins to manifest from out of thin air.[2] They do provide important information on various occult matters, such as astrology, the virtues of herbs and stones, and other arts and sciences, as well as interesting personal information on particular individuals; although none of this is actually valuable monetarily, in any legitimate manner. Additionally, one finds that any highly personal or significant information given by most of these demons, as earlier mentioned, should be taken with a grain of salt[3], depending on the source. Any data received should be well researched and validated.

There are many reasons why the magician may want to evoke goetic demons. The offices of these spirits, or specific individual magickal talents, as outlined in chapter 5, offer a myriad of possibilities open to the practitioner. These offices range from causing earthquakes to procuring love, but the most significant attributes are the ability to teach various occult arts and sciences, declare things past, present and future, and to find lost and hidden things.

These entities are also capable of attacking and destroying enemies of the operator. Be that as it may, and although the author has occasionally caused a stir or two in the occult community, and is disliked and ostracized by some, his concern is not nearly so great as to desire the painful and horrific death of any individual, nor is he capable of such animosity. Such an operation would, of course, constitute an act of the black art, as stipulated in chapter 1.

None of the materialistic offices would be worth the risk of dealing with goetic demons. The procurement of love or sex may be effectively obtained through talismanic magick and venutian invocation. The finding of treasure would be best attempted by carrying earth talismans and invoking elemental forces. An excellent familiar may be acquired by simply seeking out one's preferred kind of creature. Illness and disease should be treated by competent medical professionals.

The inevitable threat of destruction may well outweigh any likely benefits which could be obtained from the information desired, regardless of value. The physical and mental stress of the operation would be intolerable to well over 99% of the world's population. Admittedly, the author himself has been permanently affected by his evocational experiences, both positive as well as negative.

Negatively, the normal energy drain of evocation so depletes one's supply that physical deterioration seems to accelerate, and body cells actually age prematurely. Without duly preparing for literally years by a full regiment of energy building exercises, as well as physical exercise, one would almost certainly succumb to the physical stress alone. Additionally, the mental stress is sufficient to severely damage the average, or even above average psyche, and could conceivably result in a variety of disorders, of which death would appear the most merciful in comparison with the alternatives.

As severe as these possible detriments may be, the properly prepared and well educated practitioner is reasonably safe in the performance of goetic evocation. Of course, that depends on one's physical and spiritual conditioning, as well as their ability to generate an adequate supply of personal energy, properly banish elemental and planetary influences, and follow detailed instructions to the letter. The various practices outlined in the previous volume of this series, are essential to the development of the aspiring operator. These exercises, over years of frequent performance, are what makes the individual a magician, a competent practitioner capable of eventually experimenting with ritual evocation.

It should be made clear that it is rarely of necessity to perform evocationary operations of any kind. The ritual magician may never have need to practice this infernal art, and this would not make them any less the adept. The most famous ritual magicians of the nineteenth and twentieth centuries never performed a single successful goetic evocation. They may have avidly studied evocationary texts, such as the "Keys of Solomon", which was considered the primary text of ritual magick for literally centuries, and probably longer. However, neither Aleister Crowley[4], Samuel L. MacGregor-Mathers, Arthur E. Waite, Eliphas Levi, or Francis Barrett had ever publicly recorded a successful goetic evocation, resulting in the full visible appearance of the proposed spirit. This is additionally the case with any known occult scholar of present day.

The author is currently aware of no more than five living individuals capable of such a feat, only one of which is a personal acquaintance. The others, two of which apparently reside in Europe presently, have been known to produce significant effects resulting from successful evocationary operations. Their presence has been brought to the attention of the author during his experiments, albeit through somewhat questionable sources.

The desire for secrecy appears to be a strong consideration for serious practitioners of ritual evocation. There are various reasons for this, the most significant of which is self-protection from those who would attempt to coerce one to perform for another's benefit.

It should be fully understood by the aspirant that such an operation should only be performed in order to further their own spiritual and intellectual progress, and most certainly never to impress another individual, nor to prove that they possess such abilities. The primary concerns of the mature ritual magician should be the development and refinement of one's own supply of personal energy, as well as the attainment of the highest level of magickal consciousness possible. They should accept and live by the well-renowned credo of the ritual magician: "To know, to dare to will, and to keep silence.".[5]

12

NOTES ON DEMONIC PHILOSOPHY

As mentioned previously, much of the dialogue of the "Goetic" spirits was somewhat irrational, and must be taken with a grain of salt. The author has selected only the most feasible portions of their discussions to be presented here. What will be included in this chapter, is the author's personal interpretations of some of the fascinating philosophy, obtained by a few of the more cooperative spirits interrogated.

As the structure of the "human" universe is based upon and described by use of the qabalistic system, the "demonic" universe is structured according to the qliphothic system. There is a demonic plane which roughly corresponds to our terran plane[1], although it would be more accurate to describe this plane as a combination of the counterparts to our astral and terran planes together.[2] As the ninth and tenth qliphothic aspects are combined into "Giyehanim", so does the demonic terran and astral planes coexist in the same "physical" space.

The universal structure of the demonic planes is similar to that of the human universe. For basic explanatory purposes, their universe is usually considered to be "beneath" that of the human universe. In actuality, however, their universe exists as an "alternate dimension" on a parallel plane to our own. This may be described as an opposite, or the negative to our positive. Their home is essentially a negative earth, and the demons are counterparts of humans, dominating the world on which they dwell. A human could never survive there, neither physically nor astrally, and in fact, it would probably not be possible for one to voluntarily travel there astrally.[3]

The seventy-two primary Goetic demons discussed in chapter 5 are all either "fallen" angels, or spawned from the union of angels with man, therefore their life-span are indeterminate. These individuals are generally worshipped as demigods among their peers.[4]

By human standards, whose lives rarely last one century, these beings might appear to be immortal, and technically this would be an accurate assumption. They would not be considered "mortal" beings, but they will die eventually, either through injury or illness, but probably not from "natural causes", such as old age.

When summoned by ritual evocation, the demon's astral body appears, which they are adept at altering and concealing. Like our own, their physical bodies are restricted and suitable only for life on their own equivalent of our terran plane. Only the most highly evolved individual demons are capable of walking astrally among men on the terran subplane of the astral, and occasionally the lower human dream plane, sometimes interacting with human astral bodies.

In their own world, these creatures are living, breathing entities, so the term "spirit" is not altogether appropriate. However, when summoned through ritual evocation, it is their "spirit" which appears, and not their physical bodies. They are considered "evil" by humans, who consider themselves "good"; but it should be understood that these beings are essentially the opposite of humans, and may not be evil at all, depending on the perspective.

They refer to their universe as being "true", and ours as "false" or a weak impression, and in actuality, theirs was created first. They refer to humans as "light dwellers", as their world is darkened in a similar manner as to how ours is lit. It thrives on the darkness of a "black sun", which emanates the blackness of their world. This is a source of immense negative power, which exists at a great distance from their equivalent of our terran plane, where the demons' physical bodies dwell and roam free. This is an extremely foreboding place, which can be said to exist below our own dream plane, and humans may refer to it as "hell".

The coloring is predominantly grey, heavily shadowed in blackness, with some areas of dark shades of brown, red, green and blue. The visibility is said to be extremely poor, and the atmosphere is gaseous and dense, as the molecules are very close together. The landscape is mountainous and rocky. The seas are noxious and violently turbulent. No vegetation exists on their world, with the exception of a very small variety of fungi, as no sunlight is present there to support such life. Also, very little animal life is present, other than certain beasts of burden. The few species that do manage to survive independently on the demonic world would be considered horrific monsters by human standards. Additionally, a fair variety of insects do thrive there.

The natural laws of their universe are quite similar to that of the earth. Although, these creatures seem to thrive on cold, as humans do on heat. Fire is rarely used, other than in acts of destruction. The forces of gravity and magnetism are essentially identical to that of the human world. The control of electricity has apparently not been harnessed; however frequent storms produce a substantial amount of lightening, therefore it should be assumed that the potential does exist, at least in limited forms.

Their air would be considered noxious to human lungs, and the water would likewise be so to the human stomach. Their food is generally provided by certain beasts of burden and occasionally various sea creatures. It is rarely cooked, and cannibalism of the dead is considered acceptable behaviour, as well. Their diets lacks in any vegetation except for the small varieties of fungi, mentioned earlier, and this is generally only resorted to in the case of imminent starvation.

Their eyesight is conditioned for the darkness, and any light is provided by certain naturally luminescent stones and minerals. Their sense of hearing is acute, as is that of smell. These two would be considered the dominant senses. Their sense of taste is virtually non-existent. They do seem to have developed a form of effective universal telepathic communication, and the only verbal communication is that of primal grunts and screams.

Other than various large castle-like structures, mainly inhabited by the dominating factions, there are very few permanently established habitations. Most individuals and smaller groups utilize caves and temporary dwellings. They often establish villages in unoccupied areas, until driven off by a stronger dominion's military force.

The known hierarchy of the higher or dominant demons was outlined in chapters 4 and 5, as well as the numbers of legions controlled by each. These details were supposedly recorded some three thousand years ago. As would be expected, over the centuries, various changes would have occurred, and the demonic population would naturally have increased, probably vastly. At that time, the legions were said to number over 7,400,000 individuals, and these were strictly the military spirits. Demons do reproduce in a similar fashion as do humans, and it has been suggested that their current population is well over one billion, and probably closer to two billion.[5]

Their overall governing systems are monarchial in nature, although anarchism is quite prevalent, as well. There are numerous provinces and nations, several of which are dominant, tending to invade and conquer the smaller and weaker factions. Occasionally, a minor province has been successful in re-taking lost property, but frequently the smaller groups are reduced to foraging and nomadic life. These groups are culturally tribal in nature, and generally hostile towards outsiders.

Their evolution has not followed the same path as humans whatsoever. In fact, while our technology has advanced greatly over the centuries, theirs has probably digressed somewhat. Their general lifestyle has remained virtually unchanged for an extremely long period of time. The environment is extremely hostile, and survival of the fittest is the primary law of nature.

Although the technology is probably available, to a certain degree, the demonic beings have not resorted to settling their disputes with firearms, heavy artillery or weapons of mass destruction, and in this circumstance alone, they could be considered more civilized than humans.[6] Bladed weapons are frequently utilized, and their techniques of hand to hand combat are intensely savage, so much so as to be inconceivable to the human mind. Violent battles occur regularly, and certain feudal disputes have apparently been raging for literally centuries.

The dominant belief systems are basically paganistic, and several forms are practiced. Each involve relatively comparable hierarchies of corresponding "deities", although few of these would be considered especially esoteric. In fact, their systems would be considered quite primitive by human standards, or perhaps "ancient" would be the appropriate term. Only the dominant individuals seem to comprehend the integral human belief system, and are aware of the basic theories of the universe, such as "creationism" and "science".

The vast majority of the general populous would be considered somewhat uneducated, and in fact, no formal education system is utilized. Self-preservation is the primary concern.

No monetary system has been established. Wealth is measured strictly according to one's possessions and property.

Their knowledge of the physical sciences would be considered medieval by human standards. Also, their forms of art are primitive, mainly restricted to crude pottery and stone carvings.

The art of magick, which for all intensive purposes has been completely abandoned by humans, still plays an important role in the demonic culture. The dominant individuals would all be considered adept sorcerers in their own rights, and these beings have developed their magickal skills to impressive levels. In fact, those individuals likely attained their dominant status through magickal means. Usurpation and hostile takeover are the accepted manners of advancement in their monarchial hierarchy. Although this is a rather barbaric system, it is considerably straightforward when compared to the devious and unscrupulous methods utilized by the modern and "civilized" socialist politicians.

Admittedly, democracy would always be preferable over violence by the majority of the human society, it should be noted that the demonic system does possess some merits, as well as considerable detriments, as does the socialist system itself. It is a matter of social standards which determines either to be acceptable in the respective cultures. In fact, just several centuries ago, the human system was not unlike the present demonic one. Again, it is a matter of perspective.

Humans consider themselves as the "highest", most evolved species in existence; but doesn't that sound somewhat presumptuous? Are we the masters of our own destiny, or is this what we are led to believe by those who tell us what we want to hear? Do we run our own lives, or are they orchestrated by political leaders, who control our options? Does big business hamper the conversion from electrical to solar power, or the development of a fuel efficient vehicle? Does the drug industry discourage alternative medical cures of plague-like diseases, such as cancer and A.I.D.S.? Is it really necessary to pollute our environment, and expose the population to dangerous health risks? Are we indirectly responsible for the extinction of other life forms of this planet? Do we send our children to kill and die in foreign lands over matters that are plainly none of our business?

Since the answers to all of these questions rest in the affirmative, it should be apparent that we as sentient beings, are not quite so superior as we may prefer to believe. It is conceivable that other cultures might observe our actions, and be appalled by the deeds of "civilized" society.

Of course, no governmental system is perfect, and an individual person has a limited ability to effect change in their world. But before we criticize other systems, perhaps our own faults should be recognized, examined and evaluated, before passing judgement on those of foreign cultures. The philosophies of the demonic world may appear alien and disturbing to humans, but no more so than ours would appear to them.

APPENDIX A

THE TESTAMENT OF SOLOMON[1]

1. The Testament of Solomon, son of David, who was king in Jerusalem, and amstered and controlled all spirits of the air, on the earth and under the earth. By means of them, he also wrought all the transcendent works of the Temple, telling of the authorities they wield against men, and by what angels these demons are brought to naught, of the sage Solomon. Blessed art thou, O lord God, who didst give to Solomon such authority. Glory to thee and might unto the ages. Amen.

2. And behold, when the Temple of the city of Jerusalem was being built, and when the artificers were working thereat, Ornias the demon came among them toward sunset; and he took away the half of the pay of the chief-deviser's little boy, as well as half his food. He also continued to suck the thumb of his right hand every day. And the child grew thin, although he was very much loved by the king.

3. So King Solomon called the boy one day, and questioned him, saying: "Do I not love thee more than all the artisans who are working in the Temple of God? Do I not give thee double wages and a double supply of food? How is it that day by day and hour by hour thou growest thinner?"

4. But the child said to the king: "I pray thee, O king. Listen to what has befallen all that thy child hath. After we are all released from our work on the Temple of God, after sunset, when I lie down to rest, one of the evil demons comes and takes away from me the half of my pay and half of my food. Then he takes hold of my right hand and sucks my thumb. And lo, my soul is oppressed, and so my body waxes thinner every day."

5. Now when I, Solomon heard this, I entered the Temple of God, and prayed with all my soul, night and day, that the demon might be delivered into my hands, and that I might gain authority over him. And it came about through my prayer that grace was given to me from the Lord Sabaoth, by Michael his archangel. He brought me a little ring, having a seal consisting of an engraved stone, and said to me: "Take, Oh Solomon, king, son of David, the gift which the Lord God has sent thee, the highest Sabaoth. With it thou shalt lock up all the demons of the earth, male and female; and with their help thou shalt build up Jerusalem. But thou must wear this seal of God. And this engraving of the seal of the ring sent thee is a Pentalpha."

6. And I, Solomon was overjoyed, and praised and glorified the God of heaven and earth. And on the morrow I called the boy, and gave him the ring, and

said to him: "Take this, and at the hour in which the demon shall come unto thee, throw this ring at the chest of the demon, and say to him : 'In the name of God, King Solomon calls thee hither.' And then do thou come running to me, without having any misgivings or fear in respect of aught thou mayest hear on the part of the demon."

7. So the child took the ring, and went off; and behold, at the customary hour Ornias, the fierce demon, came like a burning fire to take the pay from the child. But the child, according to the instructions received from the king, threw the ring at the chest of the demon, and said: "King Solomon calls thee hither." And then he went off at a run to the king. But the demon cried out aloud saying "Child, why hast thou done this to me? Take the ring off me, and I will render to thee the gold of the earth. Only take this off me, and forebear to lead me away to Solomon."

8. But the child said to the demon: "As the Lord God of Israel liveth, I will not brook thee. So come hither." And the child came at a run, rejoicing, to the king, and said: "I have brought the demon, O king, as thou didst command me, O my master. And behold, he stands before the gates of the court of thy palace, crying out, and supplicating with a loud voice; offering me the silver and gold of the earth if I will only not bring him unto thee."

9. And when Solomon heard this, he rose up from his throne, and went outside into the vestibule of the court of his palace; and there he saw the demon, shuddering and trembling. And he said to him: "Who art thou?" And the demon answered: "I am called Ornias."

10. And Solomon said to him: "Tell me, Oh demon, to what zodiacal sign thou art subject." And he answered: "To the Water-pourer. And those who are consumed with desire for noble virgins upon earth, these I strangle. But in case there is disposition to sleep, I am changed into three forms. Whenever men come to be enamored of women, I metamorphose myself into a comely female; then I take hold of the men in their sleep, and play with them. And after a while I again take to my wings, and fly to heavenly regions. I also appear as a lion, and I am commanded by all the demons. I am offspring of the archangel Uriel, the power of God."

11. I, Solomon, having heard the name of the archangel, prayed and glorified God, the Lord of heaven and earth. And I sealed the demon and set him to work at stone cutting, so that he might cut the stones in the Temple, which, lying along the shore, had been brought by the Sea of Arabia. But he, fearful of the iron, continued and said to me: "I pray thee, King Solomon, let me go free; and I will bring you all the demons." And as he was not willing to be subject to me, I prayed the archangel Uriel to come and succor me; and I forthwith beheld the archangel Uriel coming down to me from the heavens.

12. And the angel bade the whales of the sea come out of the abyss. And he cast his destiny upon the ground, and that destiny made subject to him the great

demon. And he commanded the great and bold demon, Ornias, to cut stones at the Temple. And accordingly I, Solomon glorified the God of heaven and Maker of the earth. And he bade Ornias come with his destiny, and I gave him the seal, saying: "Away with thee, and bring me hither the prince of all the demons." So Ornias took the finger-ring, and went off to Beelzeboul, who has kingship over the demons. He said to him: "Hither! Solomon the king calls thee." But Beelzeboul, having heard, said to him: "Tell me, who is this Solomon of whom thou speakest to me?" Then Ornias threw the ring at the chest of Beelzeboul, saying: "Solomon the king calls thee." But Beelzeboul cried aloud with a mighty voice, and shot out a great burning flame of fire; and he arose, and followed Ornias, and came to Solomon.

14.   And when I saw the prince of demons, I glorified the Lord God, Maker of heaven and earth, and I said: "Blessed art thou, Lord God Almighty, who hast given to Solomon, thy servant, wisdom, the assessor of the wise, and hast subjected unto me all the power of the devil."

15.   And I questioned him, and said: "Who art thou?" The demon replied: "I am Beelzeboul, the exarch of the demons. And all the demons have their chief seats close to me. And it is I who make manifest the apparition of each demon." And he promised to bring to me in bonds all the unclean spirits. And I again glorified the God of heaven and earth, as I do always give thanks to him.

16.   I then asked of the demon if there were females among them. And when he told me that there were, I said that I desired to see them. So Beelzeboul went off at high speed, and brought unto me Onoskelis, that had a very pretty shape, and the skin of a fair-hued woman; and she tossed her hair.

17.   And when she was come, I said to her: "Tell me, who art thou?" But she said to me: "I am called Onoskelis, a spirit wrought, lurking upon the earth. There is a golden cave where I lie. But I have a place that ever shifts. At one time I strangle men with a noose; at another, I creep up from the nature to the arms. But my most frequent dwelling-places are the precipices, caves, ravines. Oftentimes, however, do I consort with men in the semblance of a woman, and above all with those of a dark skin. For they share my star with me; since they it is who privately or openly worship my star, without knowing that they harm themselves, and but whet my appetite for further mischief. For they wish to provide money by means of memory, but I supply a little to those who worship me fairly."

18.   And I Solomon questioned her about her birth, and she replied: "I was born of a voice untimely, the so-called echo of a man's ordure, dropped in a wood."

19.   And I said to her: "Under what star dost thou pass?" And she answered me: "Under the star of a full moon, for the reason that the moon travels over most things." Then I said to her: "And what angel frustrates thee?" And she said to me: "He that in thee is reigning." And I thought that she mocked me, and

bade a soldier strike her. But she cried aloud, and said: "I am subjected to thee, Oh king, by the wisdom of God given to thee, and by the angel Joel."

20. So I commanded her to spin the hemp for the ropes used in the building of the house of God; and accordingly, when I had sealed and bound her, she was so overcome and brought to naught as to stand night and day spinning the hemp.

21. And I at once bade another demon to be led unto me; and instantly there approached me the demon Asmodeus, bound, and I asked him: "Who art thou?" But he shot on me a glance of anger and rage, and said: "And who art thou?" And I said to him: "Thus punished as thou art, answerest thou me?" But he, with rage, said to me: "But how shall I answer thee, for thou art a son of man; whereas I was born an angel's seed by a daughter of man, so that no word of our heavenly kind addressed to the earth born can be overweening. Wherefore also my star is bright in heaven, and men call it, some the Wain, and some the dragon's-child. I keep near unto this star. So ask me not many things; for thy kingdom also after a little time is to be disrupted, and thy glory is but for a season. And short will be thy tyranny over us; and then we shall again have free range over mankind, so that they shall revere us as if we were gods, not knowing, men that they are, the names of the angels set over us."

22. And I, Solomon, on hearing this, bound him more carefully, and ordered him to be flogged with thongs of ox-hide, and to tell me humbly what was his name and what was his business. And he answered me thus: "I am called Asmodeus among mortals, and my business is to plot against the newly wedded, so that they may not know one another. And I sever them utterly by many calamities, and I waste away the beauty of virgin women, and estrange their hearts."

23. And I said to him: "Is this thy only business?" And he answered me: "I transport men into fits of madness and desire, when they have wives of their own, so that they leave them, and go off by night and day to others that belong to other men; with the result that they commit sin, and fall into murderous deeds."

24. And I adjured him by the name of the Lord Sabaoth, saying: "Fear God, Asmodeus, and tell me by what angel thou art frustrated." But he said: "By Raphael, the archangel that stands before the throne of God. But the liver and gall of a fish put me to flight, when smoked over ashes of the tamarisk." I again asked him, and said: "Hide not aught from me. For I am Solomon, son of David, King of Israel. Tell me the name of the fish which thou reverest." And he answered: "It is the Glanos by name, and is found in the rivers of Assyria; wherefore it is that I roam about in those parts."

25. And I said to him: "Hast thou nothing else about thee, Asmodeus?" And he answered: "The power of God knoweth, which hath bound me with indissoluble bonds of yonder one's seal, that whatever I have told thee is true.

I pray thee, King Solomon, condemn me not to go into water." But I smiled, and said to him: "As the Lord God of my fathers liveth, I will lay iron on thee to wear. But thou shalt also make the clay for the entire construction of the Temple, treading it down with thy feet." And I ordered them to give him ten water-jars to carry water in. And the demon groaned terribly, and did the work I ordered him to do. And this I did, because that fierce demon Asmodeus knew even the future. And I Solomon glorified God, who gave wisdom to me, Solomon his servant. And the liver of the fish and its gall I hung on the spike of a reed, and burned it over Asmodeus, because of his being so strong, and his unbearable malice was thus frustrated.

26.   And I summoned him again to stand before me, Beelzeboul, the prince of demons, and sat him down on a raised seat of honour, and said to him: "Why art thou alone, prince of the demons?" And he said to me: "Because I alone am left of the angels of heaven that came down. For I was first angel in the first heaven, being entitled Beelzeboul. And now I control all those who are bound in Tartarus. But I too have a child, and he haunts the Red Sea. And on any suitable occasion he comes up to me again, being subject to me; and reveals to me what he has done, and I support him."

27.   I, Solomon said unto him: "Beelzeboul, what is thy employment?" And he answered me: "I destroy kings. I ally myself with foreign tyrants. And my own demons I set on to men, in order that the latter may believe in them and be lost. And the chosen servants of God, priests and faithful men, I excite unto desires for wicked sins, and evil heresies, and lawless deeds; and they obey me, and I bear them on to destruction. And inspire men with envy, and desire for murder, and for wars and sodomy, and other evil things. And I will destroy the world."

28.   So I said to him: "Bring to me thy child, who is, as thou sayest, in the Red Sea." But he said to me: "I will not bring him to thee. But there shall come to me another demon, called Ephippas. Him will I bind, and he will bring him up from the deep unto me." And I said to him: "How comes thy son to be in the depth of the sea, and what is his name?" And he answered me: "Ask me not, for thou canst not learn from me. However, he will come to thee by my command, and will tell thee openly."

29.   I said to him: "Tell me by what angel thou art frustrated." And he answered: "By the holy and precious name of the Almighty God, called by the Hebrews by a row of numbers, of which the sum is 644, and among the Greeks it is Emmanuel. And if one of the Romans adjure me by the great name of the power Eleeth, I disappear at once."

30.   I, Solomon was astounded when I heard this; and I ordered him to saw up Theban marbles. And when he began to saw the marbles, the other demons cried out with a loud voice, howling because of their king Beelzeboul.

31.   But I, Solomon questioned him, saying: "If thou wouldst gain a respite, discourse to me about the things in heaven." And Beelzeboul said: "Hear, Oh king, if thou burn gum, and incense, and bulbs of the sea, with nard and saffron, and light seven lamps in an earthquake, thou wilt firmly fix thy house. And if, being pure, thou light them at dawn in the sun alight, then wilt thou see the heavenly dragons, how they wind themselves along and drag the chariot of the sun."

32.   And I, Solomon, having heard this, rebuked him, and said: "Silence for the present, and continue to saw the marbles as I commanded thee." And I, Solomon praised God, and commanded another demon to present himself to me. And one came before me who carried his face high up in the air, but the rest of the spirit curled away like a snail. And it broke through the few soldiers, and raised also a terrible dust on the ground, and carried it upwards; and then again hurled in back to frighten us, and asked what questions I could ask as a rule. And I stood up, and spat on the ground in that spot, and sealed with the ring of God. And forthwith the dust-wind stopped. Then I asked him, saying: "Who art thou, O wind?" Then he once more shook up a dust, and answered me: "What wouldst thou have, King Solomon?" I answered him: "Tell me what thou art called, and I would fain ask thee a question. But so far I give thanks to God who has made me wise to answer their evil plots."

33.   But the demon answered me: "I am the spirit of the ashes (Tephras)." And I said to him: "What is thy pursuit?" And he said: "I bring darkness on men, and set fire to fields; and I bring homesteads to naught. But most busy am I in summer. However, when I get an opportunity, I creep into corners of the wall, by night and day. For I am offspring of the great one, and nothing less." Accordingly I said to him: "Under what star dost thou lie?" And he answered: "In the very tip of the moon's horn, when it is found in the south. There is my star. For I have been bidden to restrain the convulsions of the hermitertian fever; and this is why many men pray to the hermitertian fever, using these three names: Bultala, Thallal, Melchal. And I heal them." And I said to him: "I am Solomon; when therefore thou wouldst do me harm, by whose aid dost thou do it?" But he said to me: "By the angel's, by whom also the third day's fever is lulled to rest." So I questioned him, and said: "And by what name?" And he answered: "That of the archangel Azael." And I summoned the archangel Azael, and set a seal on the demon, and commanded him to seize great stones, and toss them up to the workmen on the higher parts of the Temple. And, being compelled, the demon began to do what he was bidden to do.

34.   And I glorified God afresh who gave me the authority, and ordered another demon to come before me. And there came seven spirits, females, bound and woven together, fair in appearance and comely. And I, Solomon, seeing them, questioned them and said: "Who are ye?" But they, with one accord, said with one voice: "We are of the thirty-three elements of the cosmic ruler of the darkness." And the first said: "I am Deception." The second: "I am Strife." The third: "I am Klothod, which is battle." The fourth: "I am Jealousy." The

fifth: "I am Power." The sixth: "I am Error." The seventh: "I am the worse of all, and our stars are in heaven. Seven stars humble in sheen, and all together. And we are called as it were goddesses. We change our place all together, and together we live, sometimes in Lydia, sometimes in Olympus, sometimes in a great mountain."

35. So I, Solomon questioned them one by one, beginning with the first, and going down to the seventh. The first said: "I am Deception, I deceive and weave snares here and there. I whet and excite heresies. But I have an angel who frustrates me, Lamechalal."

36. Likewise also the second said: "I am strife, strife of strifes. I bring timbers, stones, hangers, my weapons on the spot. But I have an angel who frustrates me, Baruchiachel."

37. Likewise also the third said: "I am called Klothod, which is battle, and I cause the well-behaved to scatter and fall foul one of the other. And why do I say so much? I have an angel that frustrates me, Marmarath."

38. Likewise also the forth said: "I cause men to forget their sobriety and moderation. I part them and split them into parties; for strife follows me hand in hand. I rend the husband from the sharer of his bed, and children from parents, and brothers from sisters. But why tell so much to my despite? I have an angel that frustrates me, the great Balthial."

39. Likewise also the fifth said: "I am Power. By power I raise up tyrants and tear down kings. To all rebels I furnish power. I have an angel that frustrates me, Asteraoth."

40. Likewise also the sixth said: "I am Error, Oh King Solomon. And I will make thee to err, as I have before made thee to err, when I caused thee to slay thy own brother. I will lead you into error, so as to pry into graves; and I teach them that dig, and I lead errant souls away from all piety, and many other evil traits are mine. But I have an angel that frustrates me, Uriel."

41. Likewise also the seventh said: "I am the worst, and I make thee worse off than thou wast; because I will impose the bonds of Artemis. But the locust, will set me free, for by means thereof is it fated that thou shalt achieve my desire. For if one were wise, he would not turn his steps toward me."

42. So I, Solomon, having heard and wondered, sealed them with my ring; and since they were so considerable, I bade them dig the foundations of the Temple of God. For the length of it was 250 cubits. And I bade them be industrious, and with one murmur of joint protest, they began to perform the tasks enjoined.

43. But I, Solomon glorified the Lord, and bade another demon come before me. And there was brought to me a demon having all the limbs of a man, but

without a head. And I, seeing him, said to him: "Tell me, who art thou?" And he answered: "I am a demon." So I said to him: "Which?" And he answered me: "I am called Envy. For I delight to devour heads, being desirous to secure for myself a head; but I do not eat enough, but am anxious to have such a head as thou hast."

44. I, Solomon, on hearing this, sealed him, stretching out my hand against his chest. Whereon the demon leapt up, and threw himself down, and gave a groan, saying: "Woe is me! Where am I come to? Oh traitor Ornias, I cannot see!" So I said to him: "I am Solomon. Tell me then how thou dost manage to see." And he answered me: "By means of my feelings." I then, Solomon, having heard his voice come up to me, asked him how he managed to speak. And he answered me: "I, Oh King Solomon, am wholly voice, for I have inherited the voices of many men. For in the case of all men who are called dumb, it is I who smashed their heads, when they were children and had reached their eighth day. Then when a child is crying in the night, I become a spirit, and glide by means of his voice. In the crossways also I have many services to render, and my encounter is fraught with harm. For I grasp in an instant a man's head, and with my hands, as with a sword, I cut it off, and put it on to myself. And in this way, by means of a fire which is in me, through my neck it is swallowed up. It is I that sends grave mutilations and incurable on men's feet, and inflict sores."

45. And I, Solomon, on hearing this, said to him: "Tell me how thou dost discharge forth the fire? Out of what sources dost thou emit it?" And the spirit said to me: "From the Day-star. For here hath not yet been found that Elburion, to whom men offer prayers and kindle lights. And his name is invoked by the seven demons before me. And he cherishes them."

46. But I said to him: "Tell me his name." But he answered: "I cannot tell thee. For if I tell his name, I render myself incurable. But he will come in response to his name." And on hearing this, I Solomon said to him: "Tell me then, by what angel thou art frustrated?" And he answered: "By the fiery flash of lightning." And I bowed myself before the Lord God of Israel, and bade him remain in the keeping of Beelzeboul until Iax should come.

47. Then I ordered another demon to come before me, and there came into my presence a hound, having a very large shape, and it spoke with a loud voice, and said: "Hail, Lord, King Solomon!" And I, Solomon was astounded. I said to it: "Who art thou, Oh hound?" And it answered: "I do indeed seem to thee to be a hound, but before thou wast, Oh King Solomon, I was a man, that wrought many unholy deeds on earth. I was surpassingly learned in letters, and was so mighty that I could hold the stars of heaven back. And many divine works did I prepare. For I do harm to men who follow after our star, and turn them to it, and I seize the frenzied men by the larynx, and so destroy them."

48. And I, Solomon said to him: "What is thy name?" And he answered: "Staff" (Rabdos). And I said to him: "What is thine employment? And what results canst thou achieve?" And he replied: "Give me thy man and I will lead him away into a mountainous spot, and will show him a green stone, tossed to and fro, with which thou mayest adorn the Temple of the Lord God."

49. And I, Solomon, on hearing this, ordered my servant to set off with him, and to take the finger-ring bearing the seal of God with him. And I said to him: "Whoever shall show thee the green stone, seal him with this finger-ring. And mark the spot with care, and bring me the demon hither. And the demon showed him the green stone, and he sealed it, and brought the demon to me. And I, Solomon decided to confine with my seal on my right hand the two, the headless demon, likewise the hound, that was so huge; he should be bound as well. And I bade the hound keep safe the fiery spirit, so that lamps as it were might by day and night cast their light through its maw on the artisans at work.

50. And I, Solomon took from the mine of that stone 200 shekels forthe supports of the table of incense, which was similar in appearance. And I, Solomon glorified the Lord God, and then closed round the treasure of that stone. And I ordered afresh the demons to cut marble for the construction of the house of God. And I, Solomon prayed to the Lord, and asked the hound, saying: "By what angel art thou frustrated?" And the demon replied: "By the great Brieus."

51. And I praised the Lord God of heaven and earth, and bade another demon come forward to me; and there came before me one in the form of a lion roaring. And he stood and answered me, saying: "Oh king, in the form which I have, I am a spirit quite in capable of being perceived. Upon all man who lie prostrate with sickness I leap, coming stealthily along; and I render the man weak, so that his habit of body is enfeebled. But I have also another glory, Oh king. I cast out demons, and I have legions under my control. And I am capable of being received in my dwelling-places, along with all the demons belonging to the legions under me." But I, Solomon, on hearing this, asked him: "What is thy name?" But he answered: "Lion-bearer, Rath in kind." And I said to him: "How art thou frustrated along with thy legions? What angel is it that frustrates thee?" And he answered: "If I tell thee my name, I bind not myself alone, but also the legion of demons under me."

52. So I said to him: "I adjure thee in the name of the God Sabaoth, to tell me by what name thou art frustrated along with thy host." And the spirit answered me: "The 'great among men', who is to suffer many things at the hands of men, whose name is the figure 644, which is Emmanuel; it is he who has bound us, and who will then come and plunge us from the steep under water. He is noised abroad in the three letters which bring him down."

53. And I, Solomon, on hearing this, glorified God, and condemned his legion to carry wood from the thicket. And I condemned the lion- shaped one himself

to saw up the wood small with his teeth, for burning in the unquenchable furnace for the Temple of God.

54. And I worshipped the Lord God of Israel, and bade another demon come forward. And there came before me a dragon, three-headed, of fearful hue. And I questioned him: "Who art thou?" And he answered me: "I am a caltrop-like spirit, whose activity is in three lines. But I blind children in women's wombs, and twirl their ears round. And I make them deaf and mute. And I have again in my third head means of slipping in. And I smite men in the limbless part of the body, and cause them to fall down, and foam, and grind their teeth. But I have my own way of being frustrated, Jerusalem being signified in writing, unto the place called 'of the head'. For there is fore-appointed the angel of the great counsel, and now he will openly dwell on the cross. He doth frustrate me, and to him am I subject."

55. "But in the place where thou sittest, Oh King Solomon, standeth a column in the air, of purple. The demon called Ephippas hath brought it up from the Red Sea, from inner Arabia. It is he that shall be shut up in a skin-bottle and brought before thee. But at the entrance of the Temple, which thou hast begun to build, Oh King Solomon, lies stored much gold, which dig thou up and carry off." And I Solomon sent my servant, and found it to be as the demon told me. And I sealed him with my ring, and praised the Lord God.

56. So I said to him: "What art thou called?" And the demon said: "I am the crest of dragons." And I bade him make bricks in the Temple. He had human hands.

57. And I adored the Lord God of Israel, and bade another demon present himself. And there came before me a spirit in woman's form, that had a head without any limbs, and her hair was dishevelled. And I said to her: "Who art thou?" But she answered: "Nay, who art thou? And why dost thou want to hear concerning me? But, as thou wouldst learn, here I stand bound before thy face. Go then into the royal storehouses and wash thy hands. The sit down afresh before thy tribunal, and ask me questions; and thou shalt learn, Oh king, who I am."

58. And I, Solomon did as she enjoined me, and restrained myself because of the wisdom dwelling in me; in order that I might hear of her deeds, and reprehend them, and manifest them to men. And I sat down, and said to the demon: "Who art thou?" And she said: "I am called among men Obizuth; and by night I sleep not, but go my rounds over all the world, and visit women in childbirth. And divining the hour I take my stand; and if I am lucky, I strangle the child. But if not, I retire to another place. For I cannot for a single night retire unsuccessful. For I am a fierce spirit, of myriad names and many shapes. And now hither, now thither I roam. And to western parts I go my rounds. But as it now is, though thou hast sealed me round with the ring of God, thou hast done nothing. I am not standing before thee, and thou wilt not be able to command me. For I have no work other than the destruction

of children, and the making their ears to be deaf, and the working of evil to their eyes, and the binding their mouths with a bond, and the ruin of their minds, and paining of their bodies."

59. When I, Solomon heard this, I marvelled at her appearance, for I beheld all her body to be in darkness. But her glance was altogether bright and green, and her hair was tossed wildly, like a dragons; and the whole of her limbs were invisible. And her voice was very clear as it came to me. And I cunningly said: "Tell me by what angel thou art frustrated, Oh evil spirit?" But she answered me: "By the angel of God called Afarof, which is interpreted Raphael, by whom I am frustrated now and for all time. His name, if any man know it, and write the same on a woman in childbirth, then I shall not be able to enter her. Of this name the number is 640." And I Solomon having heard this, and having glorified the Lord, ordered her hair to be bound, and that she should be hung up in front of the Temple of God; that all the children of Israel, as they passed, might see it, and glorify the Lord God of Israel, who had given me this authority, with wisdom and power from God, be means of this signet.

60. And I again ordered another demon to come before me. And there came, rolling itself along, one in appearance like to a dragon, but having the face and hands of a man. And all its limbs, except its feet, were those of a dragon; and it had wings on its back. And when I beheld it, I was astonished, and said: "Who art thou, demon, and what art thou called? And whence hast thou come? Tell me."

61. And the spirit answered and said: "This is the first time I have stood before thee, Oh King Solomon. I am a spirit made into a god among men, but now brought to naught by the ring and wisdom vouchsafed to thee by God. Now I am the so-called winged dragon, and I chamber not with many women, but only with a few that are of fair shape, which possess the name of xuli, of this star. And I pair with them in the guise of a spirit winged in form, coitum habens per nates. And she on whom I have leapt goes heavy with child, and that which is born of her becomes eros. But since such offspring cannot be carried by men, the woman in question breaks wind. Such is my role. Suppose then only that I am satisfied, and all the other demons molested and disturbed by thee will speak the whole truth. But those composed of fire will cause to be burned up by fire the material of the logs which is to be collected by them for the building in the Temple."

62. And as the demon said this, I saw the spirit going forth from his mouth, and it consumed the wood of the frankincense-tree, and burned up all the logs which we had placed in the Temple of God. And I, Solomon saw what the spirit had done, and I marvelled.

63. And, having glorified God, I asked the dragon-shaped demon, and said: "Tell me, by what angel art thou frustrated?" And he answered: "By the great angel which has its seat in the second heaven, which is called in Hebrew Bazazath. And I, Solomon, having heard this, and having invoked his angel, condemned

him to saw up marbles for the building of the Temple of God; and I praised God, and commanded another demon to come before me.

64.   And there came before my face another spirit, as it were a woman in the form she had. But on her shoulders she had two other heads with hands. And I asked her, and said: "Tell me, who art thou?" And she said to me: "I am Enepsigos, who also have a myriad names." And I said to her: "By what angel art thou frustrated?" But she said to me: "What seekest, what askest thou? I undergo changes, like the goddess I am called. And I change again, and pass into possession of another shape. And be not desirous therefore to know all that concerns me. But since thou art before me for this much, hearken. I have my abode in the moon, and for that reason I possess three forms. At times I am magically invoked by the wise as Kronos. At other times, in connection with those who bring me down, I come down and appear in another shape. The measure of the element is inexplicable and indefinable, and not to be frustrated. I then, changing into these three forms, come down and become such as thou seest me; but I am frustrated by the angel Rathanael, who sits in the third heaven. This then is why I speak to thee. Yonder temple cannot contain me."

65.   I, Solomon therefore prayed to my God, and I invoked the angel of whom Enepsigos spoke to me, and used my seal. And I sealed her with a triple chain, and placed beneath her the fastening of the chain. I used the seal of God, and the spirit prophesied to me, saying: "This is what thou, King Solomon, doest to us. But after a time thy kingdom shall be broken, and again in season this Temple shall be driven asunder; and all Jerusalem shall be undone by the King of the Persians and Medes and Chaldeans. And the vessels of this Temple, which thou makest, shall be put to servile uses of the gods; and along with them all the jars, in which thou dost shut us up, shall be broken by the hands of men. And then we shall go forth in great power hither and thither, and be disseminated all over the world. And we shall lead astray the inhabited world for a long season, until the Son of God is stretched upon the cross. For never before doth arise a king like unto him, one frustrating us all, whose mother shall not have contact with man. Who else can receive such authority over spirits, except he, whom the first devil will seek to tempt, but will not prevail over? The number of his name is 644, which is Emmanuel. Wherefore, Oh King Solomon, thy time is evil, and thy years short and evil, and to thy servant shall thy kingdom be given."

66.   And I, Solomon, having heard this, glorified God. And though I marvelled at the apology of the demon, I did not credit it until it came true. And I did not believe their words; but when they were realized, then I understood, and at my death I wrote this Testament to the children of Israel, and gave it to them, so that they might know the powers of the demons and their shapes, and the names of their angels, by which these demons are frustrated. And I glorified the Lord God of Israel, and commanded the spirit to be bound with bonds indissoluble.

67. And having praised God, I commanded another spirit to come before me; and there came before my face another demon, having in front the shape of a horse, but behind of a fish. And he had a mighty voice, and said to me: "Oh King Solomon, I am a fierce spirit of the sea, and I am greedy of gold and silver. I am such a spirit as rounds itself and comes over the expanses of the water of the sea, and I trip up the men who sail thereon. For I round myself into a wave, and transform myself, and then throw myself on ships and come right in on them. And that is my business, and my way of getting hold of money and men. For I take the men, and whirl them round with myself, and hurl the men out of the sea. For I am not covetous of men's bodies, but cast them up out of the sea so far. But since Beelzeboul, ruler of the spirits of air and of those under the earth, and lord of earthly ones, hath a joint kingship with us in respect of the deeds of each one of us, therefore I went up from the sea."

68. "But I also have another character and role. I metamorphose myself into waves, and come up from the sea. And I show myself to men, so that those on earth call me Kuno Paston, because I assume the human form. And my name is a true one. For by my passage up into men, I send forth a certain nausea. I came then to take counsel with the prince Beelzeboul; and he bound me and deliver me into thy hands. And I am here before thee because of this seal, and thou dost now torment me. Behold now, in two or three days the spirit that converseth with thee will fail, because I shall have no water."

69. And I said to him: "Tell me by what angel thou art frustrated." And he answered: "By Iameth." And I glorified God. I commanded the spirit to be thrown into a phial along with ten jugs of sea-water of two measures each. And I sealed them round above with marbles and asphalt and pitch in the mouth of the vessel. And having sealed it with my ring, I ordered it to be deposited in the Temple of God. And I ordered another spirit to come before me.

70. And there came before my face another enslaved spirit, having obscurely the form of a man, with gleaming eyes, and bearing in his hand a blade. And I asked: "Who art thou?" But he answered: "I am a lascivious spirit, engendered of a giant man who died in the massacre in the time of the giants." I said to him: "Tell me what thou art employed on upon the earth, and where thou hast thy dwelling."

71. And he said: "My dwelling is in fruitful places, but my procedure is this. I seat myself beside the men who pass along among the tombs, and in untimely season I assume the form of the dead; and if I catch any one, I at once destroy him with my sword. But if I cannot destroy him, I cause him to be possessed with a demon, and to devour his own flesh, and the hair to fall off his chin." But I said to him: "Do thou then be in fear of the God of heaven and of earth, and tell me by what angel thou art frustrated." And he answered: "He destroys me who is to become Savior, a man whose number, if any one shall write it on his forehead, he will defeat me, and in fear I shall quickly retreat.

And, indeed, if any one write this sign upon him, I shall be in fear." And I Solomon, on hearing this, and having glorified the Lord God, shut up this demon like the rest.

72. And I commanded another demon to come before me. And there came before my face thirty-six spirits, their heads shapeless like dogs, but in themselves they were human in form; with faces of asses, faces of oxen, and faces of birds. And I, Solomon, on hearing and seeing them, wondered, and I asked them and said: "Who are you?" But they, of one accord with one voice, said: "We are the thirty-six elements, the world-rulers of this darkness. But, Oh King Solomon, thou wilt not wrong us nor imprison us, nor lay command on us; but since the Lord God has given thee authority over every spirit, in the air, and on the earth, and under the earth, therefore do we also present ourselves before thee like the other spirits, from ram and bull, from both twin and crab, lion and virgin, scales and scorpion, archer, goat-horned, water-pourer, and fish."

73. Then I, Solomon invoked the name of the Lord Sabaoth, and questioned each in turn as to what was its character. And I bade each one come forward and tell of its actions. Then the first one came forward, and said: "I am the first decanus of the zodiacal circle, and I am called the ram, and with me are these two." So I put them to the question: "Who are ye called?" The first said: "I, O Lord, am called Ruax, and I cause the heads of men to be idle, and I pillage their brows. But let me only hear the words, 'Michael, imprison Ruax', and I at once retreat."

74. And the second said: "I am called Barsafael, and I cause those who are subject to my hour to feel the pain of migraine. If only I hear the words, 'Gabriel, imprison Barsafael', at once I retreat."

75. The third said: "I am called Arotosael. I do harm to eyes, and grievously injure them. Only let me hear the words, 'Uriel, imprison Aratosael', at once I retreat."

76. The fifth said: "I am called Iudal, and I bring about a block in the ears and deafness of hearing. If I hear, 'Uruel, imprison Idual', at once I retreat."

77. The Sixth said: "I am called Sphendonael. I cause tumours of the parotid gland, and inflammations of the tonsils, and tetanic recurvation. If I hear, 'Sabrael, imprison Sphendonael', at once I retreat."

78. And the seventh said: "I am called Sphandor, and I weaken the strength of the shoulders, and cause them to tremble; and I paralyze the nerves of the hands, and I break and bruise the bones of the neck. And I suck out the marrow. But if I hear the words, 'Arael, imprison Sphandor', I at once retreat."

79. And the eighth said: "I am called Belbel. I distort the hearts and minds of men. If I hear the words, 'Arael, imprison Belbel', I at once retreat."

80.   And the ninth said: "I am called Kurtael. I send colics in the bowels. I induce pains. If I hear the words, 'Iaoth, imprison Kurtael', I at once retreat."

81.   The tenth said: "I am called Metathiax. I cause the reins to ache. If I hear the words, 'Adonael, imprison Metathiax', I at once retreat."

82.   The eleventh said: "I am called Katanikotael. I create strife and wrongs in men's homes, and send on them hard temper. If any one would be at peace in his home, let him write on seven leaves of laurel the names of the angel that frustrates me, along with these names: Iae, Ieo, sons of Sabaoth, in the name of the great God let him shut up Katanikotael. Then let him wash the laurel-leaves in water, and sprinkle his house with the water, from within to the outside. And at once I retreat."

83.   And the twelfth said: "I am called Saphathorael, and I inspire partisanship in men, and delight in causing them to stumble. If any one will write on paper the names of angels, Iaeo, Iealo, Ioelet, Sabaoth, Ithoth, Bae, and having folded it up, wear it round his neck or against his ear, I at once retreat and dissipate the drunken fit."

84.   The thirteenth said: "I am called Bothothel, and I cause nervous illness by my assaults. If I hear the name of the great 'Adonael, imprison Bothothel', I at once retreat."

85.   The fourteenth said: "I am called Kumeatel, and I inflict shivering fits and stupor. If only I hear the words: 'Zoroel, imprison Kumeatel', I at once retreat."

86.   The fifteenth said: "I am called Roeled. I cause cold and frost and pain in the stomach. Let me only hear the words: 'Iax, bide not, be not warmed, for Solomon is fairer than eleven fathers', I at once retreat."

87.   The sixteenth said: "I am called Atrax. I inflict upon men fevers, irremediable and harmful. If you would imprison me, chop up coriander and smear it on the lips, reciting the following charm: 'The fever which is from dirt. I exorcise thee by the throne of the most high God, retreat from dirt and retreat from the creature fashioned by God.' And at once I retreat."

88.   The seventeenth said: "I am called Ieropael. On the stomach of men I sit, and cause convulsions in the bath and in the road; and wherever I be found, or find a man, I throw him down. But if any one will say to the afflicted into their ear these names, three times over, into the right ear: 'Iudarize, Sabune, Denoe', I at once retreat."

89.   The eighteenth said: "I am called Buldumech. I separate wife from husband and bring about a grudge between them. If any one write down the names of thy sires, Solomon, on paper and place it in the ante-chamber of his house, I retreat thence. And the legend written shall be as follows: 'The God of Abram,

and the God of Isaac, and the God of Jacob commands thee - retire from this house in peace.' And at once I retire."

90. The nineteenth said: "I am called Naoth, and I take my seat on the knees of men. If any one write on paper: 'Phnunoboeol, depart Naoth, and touch thou not the neck', I at once retreat."

91. The twentieth said: "I am called Mardero. I send on men incurable fever. If any one write on the leaf of a book: 'Sphener, Rafael, retire, drag me not about, flay me not', and tie it round his neck, I at once retreat."

92. The twenty-first said: "I am called Alath, and I cause coughing and hard-breathing in children. If any one write this on paper: 'Rorex, do thou pursue Alath', and fasten it round his neck, I at once retire."

93. The twenty-third said: "I am called Nefthada. I cause the reins to ache, and I bring about dysury. If any one write on a plate of tin the words: 'Iathoth, Uruel, Nephthada,' and fasten it round the loins, I at once retreat."

94. The twenty-fourth said: "I am called Akton. I cause ribs and lumbic muscles to ache. If one engrave on copper material, taken from a ship which has missed its anchorage, this: 'Marmaraoth, Sabaoth, pursue Akton', and fasten it round the loin, I at once retreat."

95. The twenty-fifth said: "I am called Anatreth, and I send burnings and fevers into the entrails. But if I hear: 'Arara, Charara', instantly do I retreat."

96. The twenty-sixth said: "I am called Enenuth. I steal away men's minds, and change their hearts, and make a man toothless. If one write: 'Allazool, pursue Enenuth', and tie the paper round him, I at once retreat."

97. The twenty-seventh said: "I am called Pheth. I make men consumptive and cause hemorrhagia. If one exorcise me in wine, sweet-smelling and unmixed by the eleventh aeon, and say: 'I exorcise thee by the eleventh aeon to stop, I demand, Pheth (Axiopheth)', then give it to the patient to drink, and I at once retreat."

98. The twenty-eight said: "I am called Harpax, and I send sleeplessness on men. If any one write 'Kokphnedismos', and bind it round the temples, I at once retire."

99. The twenty-ninth said: "I am called Anoster. I engender uterine mania and pains in the bladder. If one powder into pure oil three seeds of laurel and smear it on, saying: 'I exorcise thee, Anoster. Stop by Marmarao', at once I retreat."

100. The thirtieth said: "I am called Alleborith. If in eating fish one has swallowed a bone, then he must take a bone from the fish and cough, and at once I retreat."

101. The thirty-first said: "I am called Hephesikireth, and cause lingering disease. If you throw salt, rubbed in the hand, into oil and smear it on the patient, saying: 'Seraphim, Cherubim, help me!' I at once retire."

102. The thirty-second said: "I am called Ichthion. I paralyze muscles and confuse them. If I hear: 'Adonaeth, help!' I at once retire."

103. The thirty-third said: "I am called Agchonion. I lie among swaddling-clothes and in the precipice. And if any one write on fig-leaves 'Lycurgos', taking away one letter at a time, and write it, reversing the letters, I retire at once. 'Lycurgos, ycurgos, kurgos, yrgos, gos, os.'"

104. The thirty-fourth said: "I am called Autothirth. I cause grudges and fighting. Therefore I am frustrated by Alpha and Omega, if written down."

105. The thirty-fifth said: "I am called Phthenoth. I cast the evil eye on every man. Therefore, the eye much-suffering, if it be drawn, frustrates me."

106. The thirty-sixth said: "I am called Bianakith. I have a grudge against the body. I lay waste houses, I cause flesh to decay, and all else that is similar. If a man write on the front-door of his house: 'Melto, Ardu, Anaath', I flee from that place."

107. And I, Solomon, when I heard this, glorified the God of heaven and earth. And I commanded them to fetch water in the Temple of God. And I furthermore prayed to the Lord God to cause the demons without, that hamper humanity, to be bound and made to approach the Temple of God. Some of these demons I condemned to do the heavy work of the construction of the Temple of God. Others I shut up in prisons. Others I ordered to wrestle with fire in the making of gold and silver, sitting down by lead and spoon. And to make ready places for the other demons in which they should be confined.

108. And I, Solomon, had much quiet in all the earth, and spent my life in profound peace, honoured by all men and by all under heaven. And I built the entire Temple of the Lord God. And my kingdom was prosperous, and my army was with me. And for the rest the city of Jerusalem had repose, rejoicing and delighted. And all the kings of the earth came to me from the ends of the earth, to behold the Temple which I built for the Lord God. And having heard of the wisdom given to me, they did homage to me in the Temple, bringing gold and silver and precious stones, many and divers, and bronze, and iron, and lead, and cedar logs. And woods that decay not they brought me, for the equipment of the Temple of God.

109. And among them also the queen of the south, being a witch, came in great concern and bowed low before me to the earth. And having heard my wisdom, she glorified the God of Israel, and she made formal trial of all my wisdom, of all the love in which I instructed her, according to the wisdom imparted to me. And all the sons of Israel glorified God.

110. And behold, in those days one of the workmen, of ripe old age, threw himself down before me, and said: "King Solomon, pity me, because I am old." So I bade him stand up, and said: "Tell me, old man, all you will." And he answered: "I beseech you, king, I have an only-born son, and he insults and beats me openly, and plucks out the hair of my head, and threatens me with a painful death. Therefore I beseech you, avenge me."

111. And I, Solomon, on hearing this, felt compunction as I looked at his old age; and I bade the child be brought to me. And when he was brought I questioned him whether it were true. And the youth said: "I was not so filled with madness as to strike my father with my hand. Be kind to me, Oh king. For I have not dared to commit such impiety, poor wretch that I am." But I, Solomon, on hearing this from the youth, exhorted the old man to reflect on the matter, and accept his son's apology. However, he would not, but said he would rather let him die. And as the old man would not yield, I was about to pronounce sentence on the youth, when I saw Ornias the demon laughing. I was very angry at the demon's laughing in my presence; and I ordered my men to remove the other parties, and bring forward Ornias before my tribunal. And when he was brought before me, I said to him: "Accursed one, why didst thou look at me and laugh?" And the demon answered: "Prithee, king, it was not because of thee I laughed, but because of this ill-starred old man and the wretched youth, his son. For after three days his son will die untimely; and lo, the old man desires to foully make away with him."

112. But I, Solomon, having heard this, said to the demon: "Is that true that thou speakest?" And he answered: "It is true, Oh king." And I, on hearing that, bade them remove the demon, and that they should again bring before me the old man with his son. I bade them make friends with one another again, and I supplied them with food. And then I told the old man after three days to bring his son again to me here: "and," said I, "I will attend to him." And they saluted me, and went their way.

113. And when they were gone I ordered Ornias to be brought forward, and said to him: "Tell me how you know this;" and he answered: "We demons ascend into the firmament of heaven, and fly about among the stars. And we hear the sentences which go forth upon the souls of men, and forthwith we come, and whether by force of influence, or by fire, or by sword, or by some accident, we veil our act of destruction; and if a man does not die by some untimely disaster or by violence, then we demons transform ourselves in such a way as to appear to men, and be worshipped in our human nature."

114. I therefore, having heard this, glorified the Lord God, and again I questioned the demon, saying: "Tell me how ye can ascend into heaven, being demons, and amidst the stars and holy angels intermingle." And he answered: "Just as things are fulfilled in heaven, so also on earth are fulfilled the types of all of them. For there are principalities, authorities, world-rulers, and we demons fly about in the air; and we hear the voices of the heavenly beings, and survey all the powers. And as having no ground basis on which to alight and rest, we lose strength and fall off like leaves from trees. And men seeing us imagine that the stars are falling from heaven. But it is not really so, Oh king; but we fall because of our weakness, and because we have nowhere anything to lay hold of; and so we fall down like lightnings in the depth of night and suddenly. And we set cities in flames and fire the fields. For the stars have firm foundations in the heaven, like the sun and the moon."

115. And I, Solomon, having heard this, ordered the demon to be guarded for five days. And after the five days I recalled the old man, and was about to question him. But he came to me in grief and with black face. And I said to him: "Tell me, old man, where is thy son? And what means this garb?" And he answered: "Lo, I am become childless, and sit by my son's grave in despair. For it is already two days that he is dead." But I, Solomon, on hearing that, and knowing that the demon Ornias had told me the truth, glorified the God of Israel.

116. And the queen of the south saw all this, and marvelled, glorifying the God of Israel; and she beheld the Temple of the Lord being built. And she gave a siklos of gold and one hundred myriads of silver and choice bronze, and she went into the Temple. And she beheld the altar of incense and the brazen which supports this altar, and the gems of the lamps flashing forth of different colours, and of the lamp-stand of stone, and of emerald, and hyacinth, and sapphire; and she beheld the vessels of gold, and silver, and bronze, and wood, and the folds of skins dyed red with madder. And she saw the bases of the pillars of the Temple of the Lord. All were of one gold, and kept apart from the demons whom I condemned to labour. And there was peace in the circle of my kingdom and over all the earth.

117. And it came to pass, while I was in my kingdom, the King of the Arabians, Adares, sent me a letter, and the writing of the letter was written as follows: "To King Solomon, all hail! Lo, we have heard, and it hath been heard unto all the ends of the earth, concerning the wisdom vouchsafed in thee, and that thou art a man merciful from the Lord. And understanding hath been granted thee over all the spirits of the air, and on the earth, and under the earth. Now, forasmuch as there is present in the land of Arabia a spirit of the following kind: at early dawn there begins to blow a certain wind until the third hour. And it's blast is harsh and terrible, and it slays man and beast. And no spirit can live upon earth against this demon. I pray thee then, forasmuch as the spirit is a wind, contrive something according to the wisdom given in the by the Lord thy God, and deign to send a man able to capture it. And behold, King Solomon, I and my people and all my land will serve thee

unto death. And all Arabia shall be at peace with thee, if thou wilt perform this act of righteousness for us. Wherefore we pray thee, condemn not our humble prayer, and suffer not to be utterly brought to naught the eparchy subordinated to thy authority. Because we are thy supplicants, both I and my people and all my land. Farewell to my Lord. All health!"

118. And I, Solomon read this epistle; and I folded it up and gave it to my people, and said to them: "After seven days shalt thou remind me of this epistle. And Jerusalem was built, and the Temple was being completed. And there was a stone, the end stone of the corner lying there, great, chosen out, one which I desired to lay in the head of the corner of the completion of the Temple. And all the workmen, and all the demons helping them, came to the same place to bring up the stone and lay it on the pinnacle of the holy Temple, and were not strong enough to stir it, and lay it upon the corner alloted to it. For that stone was exceedingly great and useful for the corner of the Temple."

119. And after seven days, being reminded of the epistle of Adares, King of Arabia, I called my servant and said to him: "Order thy camel and take for thyself a leather flask, and take also this seal. And go away into Arabia to the place in which the evil spirit blows; and there take the flask, and the signet-ring in front of the mouth of the flask, and hold them towards the blast of the spirit. And when the flask is blown out, thou wilt understand that the demon is in it. Then hastily tie up the mouth of the flask, and seal it securely with the seal-ring, and lay it carefully on the camel and bring it me hither. And if on the way it offer thee gold or silver or treasure in return for letting it go, see that thou be not persuaded. But arrange without using oath to release it. And then if it point out to the places where are gold or silver, mark the places and seal them with this seal. And bring the demon to me. And now depart, and fare thee well."

120. Then the youth did as was bidden him. And he ordered his camel, and laid on it a flask, and set off into Arabia. And the men of that region would not believe that he would be able to catch the evil spirit. And when it was dawn, the servant stood before the spirit's blast, and laid the flask on the ground, and the finger-ring on the mouth of the flask. And the demon blew through the middle of the finger-ring into the mouth of the flask, and going in blew out the flask. But the man promptly stood up to it and drew tight with his hand the mouth of the flask, in the name of the Lord God of Sabaoth. And the demon remained within the flask. And after that the youth remained in that land three days to make trial. And the spirit no longer blew against that city. And all the Arabs knew that he had safely shut in the spirit.

121. Then the youth fastened the flask on the camel, and the Arabs sent him forth on his way with much honour and precious gifts, praising and magnifying the God of Israel. But the youth brought in the bag and laid it in the middle of the Temple. And on the next day, I, King Solomon, went into the Temple of God and sat in deep distress about the stone of the end of the corner. And when I entered the Temple, the flask stood up and walked around some seven

steps, and then fell on its mouth and did homage to me. And I marvelled that even along with the bottle the demon still had power and could walk about; and I commanded it to stand up. And the flask stood up, and stood on its feet all blown out. And I questioned him, saying: "Tell me, who art thou?" And the spirit within said: "I am the demon called Ephippas, that is in Arabia." And I said to him: "Is this thy name?" And he answered: "Yes; wheresoever I will, I alight and set fire and do to death."

122. And I said to him: "By what angel art thou frustrated?" And he answered: "By the only-ruling God, that hath authority over me even to be heard. He that is born of a virgin and crucified by the Jews on a cross. Whom the angels and archangels worship. He doth frustrated me, and enfeeble me of my great strength, which has been given me by my father the devil." And I said to him: "What canst thou do?" And he answered: "I am able to remove mountains, to overthrow the oaths of kings. I wither trees and make their leaves to fall off." And I said to him: "Canst thou raise this stone, and lay it for the beginning of this corner which exists in the fair plan of the Temple?" And he said: "Not only raise this, Oh king, but also, with the help of the demon who presides over the Red Sea, I will bring up the pillar of air, and will stand it where thou wilt in Jerusalem."

123. Saying this, I laid stress on him, and the flask became as if depleted of air. And I placed it under the stone, and the spirit girded himself up, and lifted it up top of the flask. And the flask went up the steps, carrying the stone, and laid it down at the end of the entrance of the Temple. And I, Solomon, beholding the stone raised aloft and placed on a foundation, said: "Truly the Scripture is fulfilled, which says: 'The stone which the builders rejected on trial, that same is become the head of the corner.' For that it is not mine to grant, but God's, that the demon should be strong enough to lift up so great a stone and deposit it in the place I wished."

124. And Ephippas led the demon of the Red Sea with the column. And they both took the column and raised it aloft from the earth. And I outwitted these two spirits, so that they could not shake the entire earth in a moment of time. And then I sealed round with my ring on this side and that, and said: "Watch." And the spirits have remained upholding it until this day, for proof of the wisdom vouchsafed to me. And there the pillar was hanging, of enormous size, in mid air, supported by the winds. And thus the spirits appeared underneath, like air, supporting it. And if one looks fixedly, the pillar is a little oblique, being supported by the spirits; and it is so to this day.

125. And I, Solomon questioned the other spirit, which came up with the pillar from the depth of the Red Sea. And I said to him: "Who art thou, and what calls thee? And what is thy business? For I hear many things about thee." And the demon answered: "I, Oh King Solomon, am called Abezithibod. I am a descendant of the archangel. Once I sat in the first heaven, of which the name is Ameleouth. I then am a fierce spirit and winged, and with a single wing, plotting against every spirit under heaven. I was present when Moses

went in before Pharoah, king of Egypt, and I hardened his heart. I am he whom Iannes and Iambres invoked homing with Moses in Egypt. I am he who fought against Moses with wonders with signs."

126. I said therefore to him: "How wast thou found in the Red Sea?" And he answered: "In the exodus of the sons of Israel, I hardened the heart of Pharaoh. And I exited his heart and that of his ministers. And I caused them to pursue after the children of Israel. And Pharoah followed with me and all the Egyptians. Then I was present there, and we followed together. And we all came up upon the Red Sea. And it came to pass when the children of Israel had crossed over, the water returned and hid all the host of the Egyptians and all their might. And I remained in the sea, being kept under this pillar. But when Ephippas came, being sent by thee, shut up in the vessel of a flask, he fetched me up to thee."

127. I, therefore, Solomon, having heard this, glorified God and adjured the demons not to disobey me, but to remain supporting the pillar. And they both swear, saying: "The Lord thy God liveth, we will not let go this pillar until the world's end. But on whatever day this stone fall, then shall be the end of the world."

128. And I, Solomon glorified God, and adorned the Temple of the Lord with all fair-seeming. And I was glad in spirit in my kingdom, and there was peace in my days. And I took wives of my own from every land, who were numberless. And I marched against the Jebusaens, and there I saw a Jebusaean, daughter of a man; and fell violently in love with her, and desired to take her to wife along with my other wives. And I said to their priests: "Give me the Sonmanites (i.e. Shunammite) to wife." But the priests of Moloch said to me: "If thou lovest this maiden, go in and worship our gods, the great god Raphan and the god called Moloch." I therefore was in fear of the glory of God, and at first did not follow to worship.

129. But after some time, I did worship strange gods, and built great temples to Moloch and Baal and others, and I betrayed the glory of God. For this I wrote the Testament, that whomever may get it may pray for me, and attend to that which is last and not that which was first, and hence you will find grace eternal.

APPENDIX B

SOLOMONIC LORE FROM THE OLD TESTAMENT

Solomon was the son of David, who became the King of Israel in the year 1004 B.C. He was an extremely historical figure of the Old Testament and biblical folklore. Every small child of either Christian, Catholic or Jewish heritage, is told the famous story of David and Goliath, about the boy who slew the giant.

Much biographical information accompanied the detailed life of David, which makes up some forty chapters of the Old Testament, beginning in Samuel I 16:13, and ending in Kings 2:10. This was a torrid and controversial period, stories from which would make today's soap operas seem quite tame.

David was first introduced in Ruth 4:17, where his lineage is presented: "Pharez begat Hezron, and Hezron begat Ram, and Ram begat Amminadab, and Amminadab begat Nahshon, and Nahshon begat Salmon, and Salmon begat Boaz, and Boaz begat Obed, and Obed begat Jesse, and Jesse begat David.".

David was an integral part of the first book of Samuel. The conclusion of this book documents the death of Saul, then the King of Israel, who was killed in battle, as were as his three sons. Their enemies, the Phillistines, recovered the four bodies, and then cut off the King's head. They stripped off his armour, and placed it in a temple of Ashtaroth, and hung the four bodies upon the wall of Beth-shan.

The second book of Samuel depicts the events leading up to David becoming King, and then having six sons by different wives; the first son being Amnon, then Chileab, Absalom, Adonijah, Shephatiah and Ithream.

At this point in time, Amnon appears to be the immediate successor to the throne. Chileab died as a youth, leaving Absalom and Adonijah as second and third in line; however, a dramatic and incestuous event leads to the demise of the two leading heirs.

Absalom's mother, Maacah, also bore David a daughter named Tamar. Her half-brother, Amnon, lusted after and eventually raped Tamar, causing a great and understandable hatred by Absalom for Ammon. Although becoming common knowledge through gossip, Ammon was never truly punished for his crime. Being heir to the throne, he was merely "slapped on the wrist", and

179

allowed to continue in his duties. Two years after the incident, Absalom executed a pre-conceived plan, murdering Amnon, and therefore becoming a fugitive and renegade, consequently being unworthy of inheriting the throne. This left Adonijah as the rightful heir[1] However, an unexpected twist is unfolding in this sordid tale.

The Bible passages from Samuel II 11:1 through 12:24 details the events that led to the birth of Solomon.[2]

One night, King David was standing upon the roof of his palace, looking over the city of Jerusalem. From his vantage point, he saw a beautiful woman bathing through the window of her home. Her name was Bathsheba, and she was the daughter of Eliam, and the wife of Uriah the Hittite, who was an officer in the King's army. David sent his messengers to bring Bathsheba to the palace, where he seduced her. She then returned home, but later discovered that she had become pregnant. She told David about her pregnancy, and he had Uriah summoned.

The king did not tell Uriah about his conjugal actions with Bathsheba, or the pregnancy, but instead fed him well, and had his servants minister to him. He attempted to get Uriah to go home to sleep with his wife, but Uriah refused, stating "The ark, and Israel, and Judah, abide in tents; and my lord Joab, and the servants of my lord, are encamped in the open fields; shall I then go into mine house, to eat and to drink, and to lie with my wife? As thou livest, and as thy soul liveth, I will not do this thing.".[3]

The next day, David invited Uriah for dinner, and plied him with wine. Uriah got quite drunk, but the king could still not persuade him to go home to his wife. This admirable attitude led to his ultimate demise, for David then decided to have Uriah killed.

David sent a letter to Joab, his general on the battle field, and instructed him to send Uriah to the front line of the most heated battle. This ploy was successful, and Uriah was killed during the fighting. After allowing a brief time for her to mourn her husband's death, David sent for Bathsheba, and he promptly married her.

Later, Bathsheba delivered a son to David; but God was angered by his lustful and murderous actions. The child contracted a fatal sickness[4], and died. She bore a second son to David, and this child was named Solomon.

The Bible passages from Kings I 1:1 through Kings I 11:43, depicts the circumstances in which Solomon became King after David's death, and his subsequent reign. It should be noted that, although both David and Solomon were King of Israel for forty years, Solomon's life and reign was depicted in only eleven chapters, four of which were devoted exclusively to the great temples and palaces that he built. The text of the Old Testament is mysteriously lacking in substance regarding his upbringing and existence prior to becoming King, as well as personal activities while ruling.[5]

In chapter one of Kings I, David is dying of old age. His loyal servants even go so far as to bring forth a young virgin to sleep with him, hoping that would revive him; but alas, to no avail.

David's son Adonijah then attempted to usurp the throne, declaring himself as the next king. He was supported by a few of the king's generals in the upper echelon, but several of David's advisors did not join with Adonijah (most notably Bathsheba, the king's wife, Zadok the high priest, and Nathan the prophet).

Bathsheba and Nathan went before the aged David, and informed him that Adonijah was usurping the throne. Bathsheba reminded him that, previously, he had told her that Solomon should rule the kingdom after his death. After some discussion in private with Nathan, David called Bathsheba back into his chambers, and he said to her "As the Lord liveth, that hath redeemed my soul out of all distress. Even as I swear unto thee by the Lord God of Israel, saying Assuredly Solomon thy son shall reign after me, and he shall sit upon my throne in my stead; even so will I certainly do this day."[6]

So David sent for Solomon, who was still quite young, and he was crowned king.[7] When Adonijah learned that Solomon had been made king, he became afraid, for he had attempted to usurp the throne without discussing it first with David. He ran into the temple and held on to the horns of the altar. Solomon came to the temple, where Adonijah begged for his life. The new king spared his life, but this turned out to be only a temporary stay of execution. When Adonijah began to make certain demands later on, Solomon did finally have his half-brother put to death.[8]

In chapter 2 of Kings I, David passes away, and Solomon is fully established as the King. After ordering the deaths of those who opposed him (although some he merely exiled), Solomon's claim to the throne was uncontested, and also, he was in the favor of God.

In chapter three of Kings I, it is documented that Solomon made peace with the Pharoah of Egypt, and even took the pharoah's daughter as his wife. But being a child king, he did not feel that he was completely worthy of being the ruler of Israel. In the city of Gibeon, God appeared to Solomon in a dream, and offered to give him whatever he may need. He then said to God, "Thou hast shewed unto thy servant David my father great mercy, according as he walked before thee in truth, and in righteousness, and in uprightness of heart with thee; and thou hast kept for him this great kindness; that thou hast given a son to sit on his throne, as it is this day. And now, O lord my God, thou hast made thy servant king instead of David my father: and I am but a little child: I know not how to go out or come in. And thy servant is in the midst of thy people which thou hast chosen, a great people, that cannot be numbered nor counted for multitude. Give therefore thy servant an understanding heart to judge thy people, that I may discern between good and bad: for who is able to judge this thy so great a people."[9] God was pleased by Solomon's little speech, and responded by saying, "Because thou hast asked this thing, and hast not asked for thyself long life; neither hast asked for riches for thyself, nor hast asked the life of thine enemies; but hast asked for thyself understanding to discern judgement; Behold, I have done according to thy words; lo, I have given thee a wise and an understanding heart; so that there was none like thee before thee, neither after thee shall any arise like unto thee. And I have also given thee what that which thou hast not asked, both riches and honor: so that there shall not be any among the kings like unto thee all thy days. And if thou wilt walk in my ways, to keep my statues and my commandments, as thy father David did walk, then I will lengthen thy days."[10]

And so, Solomon became the wise king. The most famous bible legend concerning Solomon is documented in Kings I 3:16-28. The story begins with two women, both of which had recently given birth to sons. One child died in the night, and the mother of the dead child claimed that the living child was her own. The true mother of the child objected, and the case was brought before the king. The mothers asked him to decide which of them should raise the child. He was not able to determine which woman was lying, so he declared that the child would be divided into two sections, and each woman would get one half of the child. The first woman absurdly agreed to Solomon's "wise" descision; but the second mother begged for the life of the child, and agreed to give it up, if only he would let it live. Of course, Solomon then knew that the second woman was the true mother. The news of Solomon's judgement spread across the land, and became a testimony to his divine wisdom.

Chapter four of Kings I documents the names and lineages of the princes and officers of the royal court, as well as the perimeters of the kingdom, and the tithings that each province was required to offer. Also declared in this chapter, is that the prolific Solomon had composed three thousand proverbs, and one thousand and five songs.

Solomon was to become renowned as the builder of great temples and palaces. Chapter five and six documents the building of a great temple, which began in the fourth year of Solomon's reign. It took seven years to complete the construction. In these chapters are detailed descriptions of its dimensions, construction and ornamentation.[11]

Chapter seven documents the building of the king's palace, which took thirteen years to complete, as well as the building of the House of the Forest of Lebanon, and the house Solomon had built for his wife, the daughter of the pharoah.[12]

Chapter eight documents the deliverance of the holy ark of the covenant of the Lord[13] from Zion to the great temple of Solomon the king. Also recorded in this chapter are the lengthy prayers of Solomon, which he spoke to commemorate the new temple. In chapter nine, God speaks to Solomon for the second time, saying, "I have heard thy prayer and thy supplication, that thou hast made before me: I have hallowed this house, which thou hast built, to put my name there for ever; and mine eyes and mine heart shall be there perpetually. And if thou wilt walk before me, as David thy father walked, in integrity of heart, and in uprightness, to do according to all that I have commanded thee, and wilt keep my statues and my judgements: Then I will establish the throne of thy kingdom upon Israel for ever, as I promised to David, thy father, saying, There shall not fail thee a man upon the throne of Israel. But if ye shall turn from following me, ye or your children, and will not keep my commandments and my statues which I have set before you, but go and serve other gods, and worship them: Then will I cut off Israel out of the land which I have given them; and this house, which I have hallowed for my name, will I cast out of my sight; and Israel shall be a proverb and a byword among all people: And at this house, which is high, every one that passeth by it shall be astonished, and shall hiss; and they shall say, Why hath the Lord done thus unto this land, and to this house? And they shall answer, Because they forsook the lord their God, who brought forth their fathers out of the land of Egypt, and have taken hold upon other gods, and have worshipped them, and served them; therefore hath the Lord brought upon them all this evil.".[14]

The remainder of the chapter documents the reimbursement made to Hiram, the king of Tyre, who supplied much of the material for the building of the temple, and also, the status of the kingdom after the expense of the costly construction was expended.

In chapter ten, the famed queen of Sheba came to Israel to speak with Solomon. She had become intrigued by the tales of his great wisdom and deeds, and wanted to meet him face to face. Upon her arrival, she posed many difficult questions and riddles to the king, who answered them all correctly and immediately.[15] He made quite an impression on her, and apparently she made even more of an impression on him, for Solomon "...gave unto the queen of

Sheba all her desire, whatsoever she asked, besides that which Solomon gave her of his royal bounty.".[16]

The queen returned to her own country, and the remainder of the chapter details the wealth and treasures possessed by Solomon, and the gifts bestowed upon him by other nations. Chapter eleven is the final chapter documenting the reign of King Solomon. It records his fall from the graces of God, which was foretold in the dialogue when God spoke to him for the second time, as detailed in chapter nine. The chapters opens thusly:

> But king Solomon loved many strange women, together with the daughter of Pharoah, women of the Moabites, Ammonites, Edomites, Zidonians, and Hittites; Of the nations concerning which the Lord said unto the children of Israel, Ye shall not go in to them, neither shall they come in unto you: for surely they will turn away your heart after their gods: Solomon clave unto these in love. And he had seven hundred wives, princesses, and three hundred concubines: and his wives turned away his heart. For it came to pass, when Solomon was old, that his wives turned away his heart after other gods; for his heart was not perfect with the Lord his God, as was the heart of David his father. For Solomon went after Ashtoreth the goddess of the Zidonians, and after Milcom the abomination of the Ammonites. And Solomon did evil in the sight of the Lord, and went not fully after the Lord, as did David his Father. Then did Solomon build a high place for Chemosh, the abomination of Moab, in the hill that is before Jerusalem, and for Molech, the abomination of the children of Ammon. And likewise did he for all his strange wives, which burnt incense and sacrificed unto their gods. And the Lord was angry with Solomon, because his heart was turned from the Lord God of Israel, which had appeared unto him twice. And had commanded him concerning this thing, that he should not go after other gods: but he kept not that which the Lord commanded. Wherefore the Lord said unto Solomon, Forasmuch as this is done of thee, and thou hast not kept my covenant and my statues, which I have commanded thee, I will surely rend the kingdom from thee, and will give it to thy servant. Notwithstanding in thy days I will not do it for David thy father's sake: but I will rend it out of the hand of thy son. Howbeit I will not rend away all the kingdom; but will give one tribe to thy son for David my servant's sake, and for Jerusalem's sake which I have chosen.

The remainder of this chapter documents the rising up of Solomon's enemies, and the turmoil of the kingdom during the last years of his life.[17] Thus ends the reign of Solomon, the king of Israel.[18]

APPENDIX C

THE QLIPHOTH OF THE QABALAH[1]

These be they who be unclean and evil, even the distortion and perversion of the Sephiroth: the fallen Restriction of the Universe, the Rays of the coils of the stooping Dragon. Eleven are their classes, yet Ten are they called. Seven are the Heads, yet an Eighth ariseth. Seven are the infernal Palaces, yet do they include Ten.

In the Tree of Life, by the Waters of the River, in the Garden of Wisdom, is the Serpents of the Paths; it is the Serpent of the Celestial Eden. But the Serpent of the Temptation is that of the Tree of Knowledge of Good and Evil, the antithesis and opposer of the other: the Red coiled Stooping Dragon of the Apocalypse, the Serpent of the Terrestrial Eden. Regard thou therefore the Celestial Serpent, as of Brass, glistening with Green and Gold, the Colour of Vegetation and growth: banish thou therefore the Evil and seek the Good, thou who wouldst follow in the footsteps of our Master, Brother of the Golden Dawn. For as Moses lifted up the Serpent in the Wilderness, even so must the Son of Adam be lifted up, raise̸   ̸gh the balance of strife and of trial, through the pathway of Eternal Lif̸   ̸n, like our Master, thou art extended on that Tree, through suff̸   ̸h pain, let thy countenance be raised up towards the Ligh̸   ̸ to invoke the Divine Brightness, not for thyself, but for ̸   ̸ yet attained unto the Pathways, even though they be thy t̸

Bal̸   ̸piritual and the Material, the type of the Reconciler, remer̸   ̸f the Brazen Serpent. Mark thou well the difference bet̸   ̸ents, for before the Serpent of Brass of Numbers, the Serp̸   ̸ not stand. But at the Fall, the Serpent of Evil arising in the Tree su̸   ̸Malkuth, and linked her thus into the outer and the Qliphoth, for this is ̸   ̸n of the Fall, even the interposition of the Coils of the Stooping Dragon. Thus, therefore must Malkuth be cleansed, and this is the Redemption to come. For also Christ expiated not Sin till after he had overcome the Temptation. But surely all things in the Creation are necessary, seeing that one existeth not without the other, and the Evil also helpeth the Work, for thus the greater and more intense the Darkness, by so much the more doth the Light become bright by Contrast and draweth, as it were, increased force from the Blackness.

The Infernal Habitations:

In the first Circle are the Waters of Tears, in the second Circle are the Waters of Creation, in the third Circle are the Waters of Ocean, in the fourth Circle is the False Sea. Upon the right hand in the lesser circles are names of the Seven Earths:

1. Aretz - dry, crumbling earth

2. Adamah - reddish mould

3. Gia - undulating ground, like the side of a valley

4. Neshiah - pasture, or meadow

5. Tziah - sandy, or desert land

6. Areqa - earth

7. Thebel or Cheled - mixed earth and water

Upon the left hand are the Seven Infernal Habitations:

1. Sheol - the Depth of the Earth

2. Abaddon - Perdition

3. Titahion - The Clay of Death

4. Bar Shacheth - The Pit of Destruction

5. Tzelmoth - The Shadow of Death

6. Shaari Moth - The Gates of Death

7. Gehinnom - Hell

The Evil and Averse Powers beneath the Feet of the Four Cherubim

Lilith	The Ass	Babel
Machaloth	The Ox	Jonia
Samael	Serpents	Media
Rahab	Strange Beasts	Edom

The Mercavah

In the Mercavah Vision of Ezekial it is written: 'And I looked and behold a Whirlwind came out of the North, a great Cloud, and a Fire enfolding itself and a Splendour on every side, and Hashmal the Brilliance of the innermost flame in the midst of Fire.'

These are from Cherubic expressions of Force and the Evil and Averse Powers broken beneath their feet are: 'Rahab', whose symbol is a terrible demon leaping upon an Ox; 'Machaloth', a form compounded of a serpent and a woman, and she rideth upon a serpent scorpion; and 'Lilith', a woman outwardly beautiful but inwardly corrupt and putrefying, riding upon a strange and terrible beast. To these four (Babel, Jonia, Media, Edom) are attributed four Kingdoms, and they are also classed under the Sephiroth as shewn.

The Twelve Princes of the Qliphoth
who are the Heads of the Months of the Year

These are the names of the twelve Princes and Tribes of the Qliphoth who are the heads of the Months of the Year:

1. Bairiron - so called because they are derived from the Fourth Evil, namely Samael, the Black. Their colours are dull red and black, and their form is that of a Dragon-Lion.

2. Adimiron - whose colours are like blood mixed with water, a dull yellow and gray. Their form is that of a Lion-lizard.

3. Tzelladimiron - whose colours are like limpid blood, bronze and crimson. They are like savage triangular-headed dogs.

4. Schechiriron - whose colours are black, and their form blended of Reptile, Insect and Shell-fish, such as the crab and the lobster, yet demon-faced withal.

5. Shelhabiron - whose colors are fiery and yellow, and their form like merciless wolves and jackals.

6. Tzephariron - whose colours are like those of Earth, and their form like partially living yet decaying corpses.

7. Obiriron - whose colours are like clouds, and their form like grey, bloated goblins.

8. Necheshethiron - whose colour is like copper, and their form like that of a devilish and almost human-headed insect.

9. Nachashiron - whose colours are like serpents, and their form like dog-headed serpents.

10. Dagdagiron - whose colours are reddish and gleaming, and their form like vast and devouring flat-headed fishes.

11. Behemiron - whose name is derived from Behemoth, and their colours are black and brown, and their forms those of awful beasts like a hippopotamus, and an elephant, but crushed flat, or as if their skin was spread out flat over the body of a gigantic beetle or cockroach.

12. Neshimiron - whose colours are of a stagnant gleaming watery hue, and their forms like hideous women, almost skeletons, united to the bodies of serpents and fishes.

In the midst of the circle are placed Samael and Asmodai. The symbolic form of the former is somewhat that of the Devil of the Tarot, but colossal and attenuated; that of Asmodai is a bloated, bestial man, but in a crouching position. At the South-East Angle are placed the Evil Adam, a goat-headed skeleton-like giant; and a thousand-headed Hydra Serpent; and the Elder Lilith, the wife of Samael, a woman with an ever-changing and distorted countenance. At the North-East Angle is Aggerath, the daughter of Machalath, a fiendish with serpent hair enthroned in a chariot drawn by an Ox and an Ass. At the North-West Angle is a gigantic Scorpion with a fearful countenance, but standing upright as it were, and formed of putrefying water. After him cometh the Un-nameable one (Abaddon) and his appearance and symbol is that of a closely-veiled Black gigantic figure, covered with whirling wheels and in his hand is a vast wheel whence issue as it whirls, multitudes of cat-like demons. Behind cometh Maamah like a crouching woman with an animal's body, crawling along the ground and eating the earth. And at the South-West Angle are a winged lion and a winged horse drawing in a chariot the younger Lilith, the wife of Asmodai. She is dark, a woman to the waist and a man below it, and she appears as dragging down with her hands small figures of men into Hell.

Of the Three Evil Forces before Samael

The first is Qematriel whose form is that of a vast black, man-headed Dragon-serpent, and he uniteth under him the force of Kether of the Infernal and Averse Sephiroth. The second, a black, bloated Man-dragon, Belial, he who denieth a God; and he uniteth the force of the averse Chokmah. The third is Othiel or Gothiel, a black, bloated Man-insect, horrible of aspect, his breadth greater than his length; and he uniteth the force of the averse Binah. The fourth form is Samael the Black. All these are of gigantic nature and terrible aspect.

The Evil and Averse Sephiroth

These be the Evil and Averse Sephiroth contained in the Seven Evil Palaces, and these Sephiroth have their place from behind the holiness of the World of Assiah. And Samael the Evil surroundeth the whole Evil Sephiroth who are thus eleven instead of ten. There are eleven letters in the word 'Lieutenant Governors': Esther IX.3; eleven days from Horeb, Deut. I.2; the word 'where' in Deut. XXXII.37 is in the value eleven; eleven were the curses of Ebal; eleven were the Dukes of Edom etc. In the Evil Palaces, the first containeth Kether, Chokmah and Binah. Unto Kether is attributed Kerethial, which meaneth 'Cut off from God' (Psalm XXXVII, v.34 'When the wicked are cut off [from God]') and the symbolic form is that of black, evil Giants.

Also to Kether belong the Thaumiel or Thamiel, the Bicephalous ones; and their forms are those of dual, giant heads, with bat-like wings; they have not bodies for they are those that seek continually to unite themselves unto the bodies of other beings and forces.

Unto Chokmah are referred the Dukes of Esau and the Ghogiel (from Og, King of Bashan), or, as it is sometimes written, Oghiel, and they attach themselves unto living and material appearances, and their form is like that of the black, evil Giants with loathsome serpents twined around them. Unto Binah are referred the Satariel or Harasiel, the Concelaers and Destroyers whose forms and appearances are a gigantic, veiled head with horns and hideous eyes seen through a veil, and they are followed by evil centaurs. These are also called Seriel from Esau, because of their hairiness.

The Second Palace containeth Chesed, unto which are attributed the Gagh Shekelah, the Disturbing Ones, and their symbolic forms are those of black, cat-headed Giants. They are also called Aziel, Chazariel and Agniel. The Third Palace containeth Geburah whereunto are attributed Golaheb, or Burners with Fire, otherwise called Zaphiel, and their forms are those of enormous black heads like a volcano in eruption.

The Fourth Palace containeth Tiphareth whereunto are attributed Zamiel, and they are great black giants, ever working against each other. The Fifth Palace containeth Netzach, whereunto are attributed the Ghoreb Zereq, or Dispersing Ravens. Their form is that of hideous Demon-headed Ravens issuing from a Volcano, also called Getzphiel. The Sixth Palace containeth Hod, whereunto are referred the Samael or Deceivers (Jugglers), whose form is that of dull, demon-headed, dog-like monsters.

The Seventh Palace containeth Yesod and Malkuth. Unto Yesod are referred the Gamaliel, or Obscene Ones, whose forms are those of corrupting, loathsome bull-men, linked together. Thereunto are also referred Nachashiel, evil serpents, and Obriel. Thereunto belongeth the Blind Dragon-force. Unto Malkuth is attributed Lilith, the Evil Woman, and the appearance is that of a woman, at first beautiful but afterwards changing to a black, monkey-like demon. The name of the serpent, Nachash, hath the same number as that of Messiah, who will root out the Qliphoth from the world.

These are the Evil Chiefs:

1. Kether - Satan or Moloch

2. Chokmah - Beelzebub

3. Binah - Lucifuge

4. Chesed - Ashtaroth

5. Geburah - Asmodeus

6. Tiphareth - Belphegor

7. Netzach - Baal

8. Hod - Adramalech

9. Yesod - Lilith

10. Malkuth - Nahemah

- according to the opinion of some, but these names can hardly be referred to any one Sephira, seeing their power extendeth over many and numberless orders.

Behemoth and Leviathan are to evil forms, of which the first is the synthesis of the Qliphoth already described under the head of Behemiron in the Qliphoth of the Months of the Year (No. 11). The Leviathan are, as it were, numberless Dragon forms united together, so that each of his scales is, as it were, a separate evil serpent.

A FINAL NOTE

At the present time, the author is inclined to discontinue goetic experimentation, until such time that he is financially able to allow suitable free time for study and practice, afford the expensive texts required for continuation, and to own a proper temple away from populated areas. In today's economy, there is no telling what point in time this opportunity may present itself, if ever.

His interests have since shifted to the Enochian evocationary network, which is a much less dangerous system to work with. This will be the subject matter of the next volume of the series.

Fear not that which dwells in the darkness.

I.P.S.D.A.

- 716 -

191

NOTES

0 - INTRODUCTION

1. *The Magician's Workbook - A Modern Grimoire*, by Steve Savedow (Samuel Weiser, York Beach ME, 1995).
2. Which are in fact, invocations in reverse.
3. It is always considered a wise practice to perform a banishing upon waking, and another before going to sleep.
4. To surpass these informal suggestions is, of course, desirable.
5. Which is technically, the first book of the "Lesser Key".
6. As recorded in MacGregor-Mathers translation of "The Key of Solomon" c.1888 : Add. MSS., 10,862; Sloane MSS., 1307 & 3091; Harleian MSS., 3981; King's MSS., 288; Lansdowne MSS., 1202 & 1203.
7. Which is attributed to the infamous Aleister Crowley, but is in itself, an interesting story. See chapter 3.
8. Reportedly first published by Alibek the Egyptian, in Memphis c.1517. This grimoire is actually only reputable as far as its claim to antiquity is concerned. The text is undeniably a distorted and poorly edited rendition of the "Lesser Key".

1 - HIERARCHY

1. Websters Ninth New Collegiate Dictionary c.1989.
2. C.1909, this was listed in the previous volume as a required reference book.
3. These beings are sometimes referred to by the general species name of "Angelus Occidentalis".
4. It should be noted that some of the theory outlined here, and in future chapters, stray ever so slightly from the traditional correspondences. The author has seen fit to alter a few minor points where it seems appropriate, based on his knowledge of the subject.
5. These eight aspects would suggest the possibility for planetary attributions, and this has been suggested elsewhere in print. This theory would certainly appear highly convenient, were it not a mistaken assumption. The proper interpretation of the eight aspects are as incorporated into the four qabalistic worlds.
6. Fire signs are Aries, Leo and Sagittarius. Air signs are Gemini, Libra and Aquarius. Water signs are Cancer, Scorpio and Pisces. Earth signs are Taurus, Virgo and Capricorn.

2 - SYMBOLOGY

1. See "Gematria" by Aleister Crowley, presented in book one of "The Qabalah of Aleister Crowley" c.1973, later to be published as "777 and Other Qabalistic Writings of Aleister Crowley", and originally published in "The Equinox Volume 1, #5" c.1911.
2. The ratio of the circumference of a circle to its diameter.
3. In chapter two of Eliphas Levi's "Transcendental Magic" Its Doctrine and Rituals", first translated into English by Arthur E. Waite in 1896, Levi states "By a revolution around its own centre, the square produces a circle equal to itself, and this is the quadrature of the circle, the circular movement of four equal angles around the same point.". Waite then correctly, although rudely, dismisses this theory in a footnote, by stating "The circular movement of four equal angles around the same point has nothing to do with the problem which baffles mathematics, being the exact area of the circle. Levi is talking infantile nonsense.".
4. See appendix B of "777" by Aleister Crowley, c. 1909. Also see chapter one, verse four of "The Book of the Law" by Crowley, c.1904.
5. The geometrical figure consisting of three points connected by three lines of equal length, with the apex pointing upwards.
6. See Diagram #2.
7. See "The Mystical Qabala" chapter 8, c.1935.
8. See Diagram #3.
9. See Diagram #4.
10. Satanists consider "indulgence" as their primary and supreme virtue.
11. "Mystical Qabala" chapter 8, c.1935.
12. A richly embroidered outer vestment.
13. See Book 2, chapter 11 of Agrippa's "Three Books of Occult Philosophy", c.1531.
14. See Book 2, chapter 12 of Agrippa's "Three Books of Occult Philosophy", c.1531.
15. As will be discussed in chapter four.
16. Taken from "The Key of Solomon", translation by S.L. MacGregor-Mathers, C.1888.

3 - A BRIEF HISTORY OF "THE KEY OF SOLOMON"

1. C.1987.
2. The exception to this rule is of course, Egyptian papyrus, which was specifically treated in order to increase its longevity.
3. C.1957.
4. Published in Madrid 1942.

5. Also see appendix A.
6. First published in French, c.1929, and translated to English by J. Courtenay Locke, in 1931. This chapter includes some fascinating Solomonic lore, taken from early texts, such as "Das Buch Belial" by Jacobus de Teramo, c.1473. This book is highly recommended reading.
7. See appendix B.
8. A pseudonym for Alphonse Louis Constant, 1810-1875. The book noted was translated from the French by Arthur E. Waite, c.1913.
9. C. 1911, a revised and expanded edition of "The Book of Black Magic and Of Pacts", first published in 1898.
10. C.1889.
11. Even though sufficient warning was established in the introduction.
12. Waite was unfortunately rather critical of everything which he disagreed with, or what he determined to be questionable. He went so far as to actually ridicule Eliphas Levi in the footnotes of Levi's own texts, which Waite translated, rather than keeping his insulting commentary to himself. This was undoubtedly the root for the hatred Aleister Crowley harbored for Waite, as Crowley believed himself to be Levi, in his previous incarnation. (See "Magick in Theory and Practice", chapter 7, section 6.) In example, Crowley made specific note to Waite in his introductory essay to the 1904 translation of "The Goetia", as follows: "Ah! Mr. Waite, the world of Magic is a mirror, wherein who sees muck is muck.".
13. John Weirus or Johann Weyer, 1515-1588, a Belgian physician and demonologist, who studied under Cornelius Agrippa for a time.
14. The "other sections" refers to the second part or "Theurgia Goetia", the third part or "Pauline Art", the fourth part or "Almadel", and the fifth part or "Notary Art".
15. Being references in highly reputable early manuscripts, records of experiments by ritual practitioners detailing successful results obtained by operations outlined therein, not to mention the sheer intricate detail of the system itself.
16. Published by the Society for the Propagation of Religious Truth, c.1904.
17. C.1977.
18. This was reprinted in coordination with Samuel Weiser Publishing Co. in 1992.

4 - THE QLIPHOTH

1. C.1888.
2. C.1935.
3. C.1965.

4. See appendix C.
5. C.1912.
6. Edited by Israel Regardie, c.1974.
7. C.1976.
8. Or Frater Achad, as he was better known.
9. C.1925.
10. C.1922.
11. C.1977.
12. C.1975.
13. C.1980.
14. C.1992.
15. The association between Samael and Satan is a common biblical misinterpretation, which will be briefly discussed shortly.
16. C.1927.
17. Powell earlier described a shade as being a dead person's "astral corpse", in its earliest stages of disintegration.
18. See chapter 9 in the previous volume of this series.
19. Being Ain, Ain Soph, and Ain Soph Aur.
20. Which corresponds to Kether.
21. The three correspond to the Father, Son and the Holy ghost, qabalistically.
22. Which corresponds to Chokmah.
23. Which refers to the attraction of flies to death and putrefaction.
24. Which corresponds to Binah.
25. This is said to have been first printed in the seventeenth century, and includes "the infernal devices of the great Agrippa for the discovery of all hidden treasures and the subjugation of every denomination of spirits, etc.". A French translation was also published in the early nineteenth century as "Le Dragon Rouge" or "The Red Dragon", boasting a fictitious copyright date of 1522.
26. It would prove to be a most "grand" error in judgement for any practitioner to attempt an evocation of any of these demon kings. Their energy could easily overcome all but the most powerful of ritual magicians.
27. The Goetic demons will be discussed extensively in the next chapter.
28. Which corresponds to Chesed.
29. Which corresponds to Geburah.
30. Which corresponds to Tiphareth.
31. Which corresponds to Netzach.
32. Which corresponds to Hod.
33. Which correspond to Yesod and Kether.
34. It should be needless for the author to remind the practitioner, that they should perform banishing rituals before and after each experiment. Also, all astral magickal weapons should be carried.

5 - THE GOETIC DEMONS

1. This word has a numerical value of 971, and is interpreted as the "divided name" of God.
2. As mentioned in chapter 3, Furcas then assumed Belial's former position. It appears that a tiny bit of the author's conjecture did slip in.
3. i.e.: kings - solar, prince - Jupiter, duke - Venus, knight - Saturn, earl - Mars, marquis - lunar, president - Mercury.
4. The author initially utilized Aleister Crowley's "777" and "Sepher Sephiroth" as references for these charts; however, he discovered the data to be riddled with error. The student is encouraged to compare these charts with those in Crowley's texts, and determine for themselves which appear to be the most accurate.
5. A few of the names vary slightly with the different manuscripts. The names presented here are the generally accepted variations.
6. Again, the numbers of legions quoted vary slightly in the different manuscripts.

6 - PREPARATIONS FOR GOETIC EVOCATION

1. The results of evocation are discussed in chapter 11 of this volume, which may well be the most important section of this text.
2. "It is one great mistake of the beginner to concentrate his force upon the actual stated purpose of the ceremony. This mistake is the most frequent cause of failures in invocation." Aleister Crowley, "Magick in Theory and Practice", chapter XV (c. 1929).
3. See description of circle used by the author, chapter eight of this volume.
4. MacGregor-Mather's translation, c.1888. Conveniently, the majority of this procedure was recorded in chapter 2 of the first volume of this series.
5. Of course, substituting the words and symbols illustrated in diagram #9.
6. Air - east, fire - south, water - west, earth - north.
7. See the description of the triangle in chapter eight of this volume.
8. Cinnabar is artificial red mercuric sulfide, and may be obtained from art supply outlets.
9. These may be engraved on to the blade, but it is also permissible to paint them on using properly purified and consecrated black acrylic paint. If painted on, the blade should be cleaned immediately after the operation, and re-painted just before the next.
10. The capitalized names in this and the other prayers presented here, should be vibrated, as described in chapter 5 of the previous volume.

11. The cloth should be kept in a wooden box full of sweet spices for seven days after purchasing, purifying and consecrating.
12. Engraved or painted, as the dagger.
13. Sigils of kings must be of gold, the duke's are of copper, the prince's are of tin, the marquise's are of silver, the president's are of a combination silver and copper, the knight's are of lead, and the earl's are of iron.
14. It is permissible to use properly prepared ink or paint.
15. As should by now be understood, every thing having the remotest connection to magickal practices should be duly prepared by purification and consecration. This includes such minor accessories as pens and brushes used to make sigils, as well as the ink and paint itself. Included as well is the incense and censer, the hyssop used to treat the water, and also the paper, parchment and notebooks used to keep information or record events.
16. Also, previously to the ritual bathing, all electrical outlets in the general area of the operation should be cleared of any plugs, and the fuses or circuit breakers removed. For some unknown reason, the act of Goetic evocation somehow generates electricity, or more likely, increases either the voltage or amperage of exposed current. (Loosely defined, voltage is the potential amount of electricity flowing between two points in a wire, and amperage refers to the strength or intensity of the current.) In any event, the apparent result of exposing electrical current to an evocationary operation is an extreme power surge, which may well burn up anything connected to the circuit. During the authors first successful evocation, a wall unit air conditioner, several lamps and small appliances were destroyed due to electrical overload. Fortunately, the circuit breakers of the dwelling were divided by room, and the rest of the house was not affected. However, one of the room's breakers melted in its slot, and the other was physically forced out of its slot, actually denting the door of the circuit box, and lay loose in the bottom of the box.

7 - THE PERFORMANCE

1. The back of the altar should be hollow. This is partly to provide a place for the two notebooks, one of which contains the written conjurations, which may be required for reference, and the other to record any dialogue and experience during the operation. Two new and properly prepared pens should also be available.
2. First three times, pause, four times, pause, and then three times.
3. See chapter 3 of volume one.
4. As outlined in chapter 5 of the preceding volume.
5. As outlined in appendix C of the preceding volume.

6. All conjurations, etc. are presented in section B of this chapter.

7. It manifests in a manner which excites several human instincts, most notably fear, apprehension, and anxiety, to name a few. These natural human reactions are quite normal; but unfortunately, they can also instigate disastrous results, if they should distract the operator at a crucial moment. It is important for the magician to expect these reactions, and prepare accordingly, teaching oneself to suppress these emotional regressions, at least during ritual.

8. It would not be objectionable to make several attempts before resorting to the curses, especially in the case of the very first attempts by the practitioner. However, it has been the author's experience that an obstinate spirit may resist indefinitely without considerable threatening and torment.

9. Remember to shut the lid of the box, so no fumes disturb the proceedings.

10. "Let him beware of the 'lust of result', of expecting too much, of losing courage if his first success is followed by a series of failures. For success makes success seem so incredible that one is apt to create an inhibition fatal to subsequent attempts. One fears to fail; the fear intrudes upon the concentration and so fulfils its own prophecy." Aleister Crowley, "Liber Samekh: Theurgia Goetia Summa (Congressus Cum Daemone) sub figura DCCC.", appendix IV of "Magick in Theory and Practice".

11. One should not have to wait for visual appearance. Their presence will become noticable previous to full manifestation.

12. A partial manifestation should be considered adequate for the operator's first successful evocations.

13. The sword should be in the right hand, pointing at the spirit, if righthanded. If lefthanded, it is permissible for the sword to be in the left, and use the right hand to extend the pentacle. Also, the author found it appropriate to continue holding the protective disk, and using that hand, lift the pentagram from your chest with the uppermost edge of the disk, leaning forward slightly, to point the disk at the spirit.

14. Meaning that in certain situations, the specific demon summoned may not always be the one that appears.

15. Such as in chapter XVI, part II of Aleister Crowley's "Magick in Theory and Practice", where he does add: "The precaution indicated is not to let oneself sink into one's humanity while the weapon is extended beyond the circle. Were the force to flow from it to you instead of from you to it, you would be infallibly blasted, or, at the least, become the slave of the spirit.".

16. The conjurations, etc. presented in section B of this chapter have been taken directly from the "Goetia", being the well known English translation of 1904, with some minor editing by the author.

17. All capitalized words should be vibrated.

8 - GOETIC EXPERIMENTS #1 - #5

1. Plywood was used so as not to permanently affect the flooring of the rented dwelling.
2. Or even in the upper planes, where the author has regularly traveled and explored for several years previously to these proceedings.

9 - GOETIC EXPERIMENTS #6 - #8

1. These may have been partly affected by a slight apprehension on both of our parts, which we discussed openly after the unsuccessful experiments.
2. The box we used was a black steel file box, of the common variety used to hold 3 x 5 cards.

10 - GOETIC EXPERIMENT #9

1. They had both previously memorized the release and closing from the "Lesser Key", as part of the initial preparation period in early 1985.
2. The shields as described in chapter 6, marked with three rings and words of power, being TETRAGRAMMATON, ANAPHAXETON, AND MICHAEL.
3. The triangle being elevated, the total height was approximately nine feet from floor level.
4. I had not looked back to observe S.H. or his actions, although in later discussion, his descriptions of the events we both experienced matched almost identically. A few minor discrepancies were noted, and later attributed to our individual perspectives.
5. The author is 5'9".
6. It should be noted that all dialogue following here and in future chapters was hastily recorded by S.H. during the ritual. The author used these as reference afterwards, when recording the events in his personal journal, supplementing his own recollection of the events.
7. The author later scrutinized and studied these in sequence, which led to conclusions of a highly personal nature.
8. S.H. did hear the voice also, recording the dialogue quite efficiently. Only extremely minor discrepancies were noted between our experiences.
9. After a bit more rhetoric, the spirit does confess his "secret name". The author here deems fit to exclude this name from the text. It is of utmost importance that the practitioner personally compels their prisoner to convey this name, without having knowledge of it in advance. On the

other hand, once obtained the operator may re-evoke the spirit with ease, theoretically after only reciting the first conjuration. Since nothing in life comes easily, the author declines to divulge this spirit's name here. The dialogue presented continues immediately after the spirit reveals its secret.

10. This reflection was all conjecture, considered by the author at the time, with no evidence or testimony to substantiate.

11 - THE RESULTS

1. Of course, they were not aware of the experiments.
2. It is the loosest of speculation by the author that the supposed author of this grimoire, Solomon, who was at the time King of Israel, may have been capable of obtaining the possessions of an individual who has died. Therefore, a demon could conceivably have killed a wealthy person for Solomon, and he would then usurp their fortune.
3. Or the whole shaker, in some cases.
4. According to Gerald Yorke, in the biographical introduction of "A Bibliography of the Works of Aleister Crowley"(c.1991), Crowley had "...only once succeeded in evoking a demon (Buer) to partial appearance.".
5. "His angel shall lead him anon to the summit of the Order of the R.C. and make him ready to face the unspeakable terror of the Abyss which lies between Manhood and Godhead; teach him to Know that agony, to Dare that destiny, to Will that catastrophe, and to keep Silence for ever as he accomplishes the act of annihilation." Aleister Crowley, "Magick in Theory and Practice", appendix II.

12 - NOTES ON DEMONIC PHILOSPHY

1. See chapter 8 of the previous volume.
2. These creatures are that what human nightmares are made of, however they have no dreams of their own. In fact, their physical bodies do not require sleep at all, as human bodies do.
3. Theoretically, a supreme adept may be capable of traveling "downward" to the demonic planes, however this might be considered an attempt at "astral suicide", due to the enormous danger factor. The chances of surviving the experience to return to their physical body would be slim, at best.
4. The demons born from two demons have an average life-span of approximately one hundred and fifty years. Due to the conditions of

their world, which will be discussed shortly, diseases are rare, as few living viruses and germs are capable of surviving there.

5. Obviously, these creatures are divided by gender as males and females, capable of sexual reproduction.
6. It is true, however, that their world is quite barren, and only a few individuals are capable of refining what little metals are obtainable.

APPENDIX A - THE TESTAMENT OF SOLOMON

1. The folowing version of "The Testament of Solomon" was translated from a Greek manuscript by Frederick Conybeare, and was published in "The Jewish Quarterly Review, Volume 11" (London: 1898).

APPENDIX B - SOLOMONIC LORE FROM THE O. T.

1. Although Absalom still made claim to that status, albeit from a distance.
2. The rape of Tamar was actually depicted in Samuel II, chapter 13, just after the birth of Solomon.
3. Samuel II 11:11.
4. Presumably, by the hand of God.
5. His magical exploits are well documented, however, in various ancient Hebraic and Arabic literature and folklore.
6. Kings I 1:29-30.
7. This occured in 965 B.C.
8. In Kings I 2:24-25.
9. Kings I 3:6-9
10. Kings I 3:11-14.
11. In fact, there have been several books written over the last few centuries exclusively about the building of this temple.
12. The dimensions of the great temple, as well as the other palaces and houses built by Solomon, are said to have great qabalistic significance, as do the details of the ornamentation, which are thoroughly described in these chapters (for instance, the descriptions of the pillars of Jachin and Boaz). The in-depth investigation of these details make quite an illuminating qabalistic study.
13. Which is said to contain the tablets of the commandments of God.
14. Kings I 9:3-9.
15. Although not recorded in the Old Testament, the questions asked by the queen of Sheba are documented in "The Targum to Esther" (The most notable publications of this book are the 1885 Leipzig edition, edited by P. Cassel, and the 1898 Berlin edition, edited by E. David) and "The

Midrash to the Proverbs" (The most notable publications of this book are the 1885 edition, edited by A. Wunsche, and the 1893 edition, edited by S. Buber.).

16. Kings I 10:13.
17. An interesting note is made in Kings I 11:41: "And the rest of the acts of Solomon, and all that he did, and his wisdom, are they not written in the book of the acts of Solomon?". Although there are several known books attributed to Solomon, such as "The Testament of Solomon" (see appendix A), "The Odes of Solomon" and "The Psalms of Solomon" (both of which have been translated into English, and published in "The Forgotten Books of Eden" (World Publishing Co.; Cleveland: 1927.), "The Key of Solomon" (London: 1888), "Goetia: The Lesser Key of Solomon" (Boleskine: 1904), etc.; however, nothing is known of "the book of the acts of Solomon" mentioned in this passage.
18. Solomon's son, Rehoboam, was made King after his death. In fact, the "Key of Solomon the King" was apparently written by Solomon for his son, as mentioned in the MacGregor-Mather's translation. Rehoboam's reign was marred by the subsequent division of the kingdom, due to his lack of diplomatic skills, and lasted only seventeen years. This was documented in just three chapters of Kings I (Chapter 12 - chapter 14.). Interestingly enough, in Kings I 14:29, the passage reads, "Now the rest of the acts of Rehoboam, and all that he did, are they not written in the book of the chronicles of the Kings of Judah?".

APPENDIX C - THE QUIPHOTH OF THE QABALAH

1. This essay was originally an instructional paper for initiates of the Isis-Urania temple of the Golden Dawn, transcribed circa 1900. This has been re-published in "The Sorcerer and His Apprentice", edited by R.A. Gilbert, in the "Roots of the Golden Dawn" series, c.1983. Also, the recent edition of "The Grimoirium Verum", published by Trident Press in 1994, includes an appendix entitled "Booke of the Black Serpent", which is actually an edited and supplemented trasncription of this qliphothic essay.